Facebook® & Twitter® For Seniors
FOR DUMMIES®

by Marsha Collier

WILEY

John Wiley & Sons, Inc.

Facebook® & Twitter® For Seniors For Dummies®

Published by
John Wiley & Sons, Inc.
111 River Street
Hoboken, NJ 07030-5774
www.wiley.com

Copyright © 2010 by John Wiley & Sons, Inc., Hoboken, New Jersey

Published by John Wiley & Sons, Inc., Hoboken, New Jersey

Published simultaneously in Canada

For general information on our other products and services, please contact our Customer Care Department within the U.S. at 877-762-2974, outside the U.S. at 317-572-3993, or fax 317-572-4002.

For technical support, please visit www.wiley.com/techsupport.

Wiley publishes in a variety of print and electronic formats and by print-on-demand. Some material included with standard print versions of this book may not be included in e-books or in print-on-demand. If this book refers to media such as a CD or DVD that is not included in the version you purchased, you may download this material at http://booksupport.wiley.com. For more information about Wiley products, visit www.wiley.com.

Library of Congress Control Number: 2010933459

ISBN: 978-0-470-63754-8 (pbk); ISBN: 978-0-470-92077-0 (ebk); ISBN: 978-0-470-92078-7 (ebk); ISBN: 978-0-470-92079-4 (ebk)

Manufactured in the United States of America

10 9 8 7 6

WILEY

About the Author

Marsha Collier spends a good deal of time online. She loves buying and selling on eBay, as well as meeting online denizens from around the world. As a columnist, author of the best-selling *For Dummies* books on eBay, and a radio host, she shares her knowledge of the online world with millions. Before her eBay career took off, Marsha owned and operated her own marketing and advertising firm, a company that won numerous awards and earned her "Small Business of the Year" accolades from several organizations. She got started online during the Internet's early years, and quickly mastered the art making friends online.

Marsha is one of the foremost eBay experts and educators in the world — and the top-selling eBay author. In 1999, Marsha created the first edition of *eBay For Dummies*, the bestselling book for eBay beginners. Then she followed up the success of the first book with *Starting an eBay Business For Dummies*, targeting individuals interested in making e-commerce their full-time profession. That book became an instant nationwide hit, making several notable bestseller lists.

Currently, Marsha has 20 books in print on her favorite subject — eBay. Her *eBay For Dummies* was published in special versions for the United Kingdom, Canada, Germany, China, France, Spain, and Australia. Marsha's books have sold over 1,000,000 copies (including the special editions in foreign countries as well as translations in Spanish, French, Italian, Chinese, and German). These books are updated regularly to keep up with site and market changes.

Along with her writing, Marsha is an experienced e-commerce educator. She was the lead instructor at eBay University (teaching seminars all over the United States), as well as a regular presenter at the eBay Live national convention since its inception. Marsha also hosted "Make Your Fortune Online," a PBS special on online business that premiered in 2005. The show was the basis for her PBS premium five-DVD set, "Your Online Business Plan." In 2006, she was invited to address the Innovations Conference in Singapore to present the ideas of e-commerce to a new market.

In 2008, she was dubbed one of twenty influential iCitizens in Kelly Mooney's *The Open Brand: When Push Comes to Pull in a Web-Made World*, and was invited to speak at a leading e-commerce conference attended by Coca-Cola, Hewlett Packard, Procter & Gamble, Victoria's Secret, and other e-commerce leaders.

She hosts Computer & Technology Radio on KTRB 860 AM in San Francisco, as well as on the Web at `www.computerandtechnology radio.com`. She also makes regular appearances on television, radio, and in print to discuss customer needs and online commerce.

Marsha currently resides in Los Angeles, CA. She can be reached via her Web site, `www.marshacollier.com`.

Dedication

To all the future online citizens who have purchased this book to get a taste of how much fun joining the online party can be. I look forward to seeing you on Twitter and Facebook, hearing your stories, and learning from you.

I dedicate this book also to my daughter, Susan Dickman, who's always been there to help me get "cool." Heather Meeker, who's there with support and love — thank you. And to my dear friends on Twitter and Facebook who have embraced me as part of their community, I want to thank all of you for your help and support; you make the online world a fun place to visit for millions of people. Keep on doing what you're doing.

Author's Acknowledgments

This book couldn't have been written without input from the thousands of wonderful people that I've met online from all over the world. You inspire me to work harder and do my best to help as many people as possible.

I've made so many friends along my eBay, Facebook, and Twitter travels: If not for them, this book wouldn't be here. Thanks to the rest of my Twitter buddies — who always seem to have a lightning-fast response when I send them a tweet.

I particularly want to thank my freaking brilliant editors at Wiley Publishing, Inc. who helped make this book as much fun as it is: my über-smart project editor Leah Cameron, my super editor Barry Childs-Helton, and my tech editor Mark Justice Hinton; Steven Hayes, my acquisitions editor, who is always there for supports and ideas; and Andy Cummings, my publisher, who — lucky for me — still takes my calls!

Thank you all!

Publisher's Acknowledgments

We're proud of this book; please send us your comments through our online registration form located at http://dummies.custhelp.com. For other comments, please contact our Customer Care Department within the U.S. at 877-762-2974, outside the U.S. at 317-572-3993, or fax 317-572-4002.

Some of the people who helped bring this book to market include the following:

Acquisition and Editorial

Senior Editorial Manager: Leah P. Cameron

Senior Copy Editor: Barry Childs-Helton

Acquisitions Editor: Steven Hayes

Technical Editor: Mark Justice Hinton

Editorial Assistant: Amanda Graham, Leslie Saxman

Sr. Editorial Assistant: Cherie Case

Cartoons: Rich Tennant (www.the5thwave.com)

Composition Services

Project Coordinator: Patrick Redmond

Layout and Graphics: Carrie A. Cesavice

Proofreaders: Melissa Cossell, Evelyn C. Wellborn

Indexer: Sharon Shock

Publishing and Editorial for Technology Dummies

    Richard Swadley, Vice President and Executive Group Publisher

    Andy Cummings, Vice President and Publisher

    Mary Bednarek, Executive Acquisitions Director

    Mary C. Corder, Editorial Director

Publishing for Consumer Dummies

    Kathleen Nebenhaus, Vice President and Executive Publisher

Composition Services

    Debbie Stailey, Director of Composition Services

Contents at a Glance

Introduction 1

Part I: Computer and Internet Basics 9
Chapter 1: Getting a Computer Ready for the Internet.................11
Chapter 2: Hooking Up to the Internet.....................................27
Chapter 3: All About E-Mail...43
Chapter 4: Speaking the Social Networking Language....................63

Part II: Putting Your Face onto Facebook 77
Chapter 5: Preparing Your Facebook Profile 79
Chapter 6: Preparing to Share Info...97
Chapter 7: Connecting with Friends and Family........................ 115
Chapter 8: Adding Photos and Videos to Facebook..................... 137
Chapter 9: Exploring Groups, Events, and Games 153

Part III: And Now, It's Twitter Time 181
Chapter 10: A Beginner's Guide to Twitter 183
Chapter 11: Conversing on Twitter with Friends, Family, and More.............. 203
Chapter 12: Gathering Tools of the Twitter Trade...................... 215

Part IV: The Rest of the Social Networking Story 239
Chapter 13: Sharing (and Grabbing) Photos, Videos, and Music.................... 241
Chapter 14: Giving or Taking an Opinion................................. 263
Chapter 15: So You Want to Be a Blogger?............................... 285

Index.. 305

Table of Contents

Introduction 1

    About This Book 3

    Conventions Used in This Book 4

    Foolish Assumptions 5

    How This Book Is Organized 6

    Where to Go from Here 7

    Feedback, Please 8

Part 1: Computer and Internet Basics 9

    Chapter 1: Getting a Computer Ready for the Internet 11

        Pick Hardware to Match Your Computer Use 12

        Know What Hardware Options to Look For 16

        Shop for Your Computer of Choice 19

        Browse for a Browser 21

    Chapter 2: Hooking Up to the Internet 27

        Select an Internet Service Provider 28

        Set Up a Dial-Up Connection 31

        Choose a Broadband Network Option 32

        Connect a Powerline Network 34

        Connect a Wireless Network 36

        Remember These Rules to Stay Safe Online 41

    Chapter 3: All About E-Mail 43

        Check Out Places to Get Your E-Mail Service 44

        Meet the Big Three Web-Based E-Mail Providers 46

        Pick a Pick-Proof Password 51

        Sign Up for a Gmail Account 52

        Add Your Contacts 57

        Compose and Send an E-mail 59

Chapter 4: Speaking the Social Networking Language 63

Gather on Facebook..64

Communicate through Twitter...66

Find a Spot on MySpace 68

Get Connected on LinkedIn 69

See It All on YouTube 70

Have Your Say on BlogSpot 71

Share Photos on Flickr 73

Stream Music on Pandora 73

Watch TV and Movies on Hulu..75

Part II: Putting Your Face onto Facebook **77**

Chapter 5: Preparing Your Facebook Profile.................... 79

Sign Up for a Facebook Account..80

Find Friends Initially...82

Add Your Personal Information..84

Upload Your Profile Photo..85

Confirming You Are You 90

Fill Out Other Profile Information 91

Go Back to Edit Your Profile Later..96

Chapter 6: Preparing to Share Info................................ 97

Get Your Privacy and Security Settings in Place.....................98

Meet Your Facebook Home Page.. 102

Review Your Timeline Page 104

Update Your Status 109

Delete a Status Update or Other Post.................................... 110

Add a Photo to Your Timeline 111

Adding Timeline Life Events 112

Share a YouTube Video on Facebook..................................... 113

Chapter 7: Connecting with Friends and Family 115

Make the Navigation Bar Your First Stop 116
Find a Friend with Facebook Search 118
Send a Friend Request 121
Find Friends in Other Friends' Lists 122
Respond to a Friend Request 123
Connect with a Facebook Network 125
Send Private Messages to Friends 127
Retrieve a Private Message 129
Chat with Your Friends 130
Post Updates on a Friend's Wall 132
Comment on a Friend's Status 134
Post a Note 135
Remove Messages from Your Wall 136

Chapter 8: Adding Photos and Videos to Facebook 137

Upload a Photo to Your Account 137
Create a Photo Album 141
Tag Photos 146
Untag Yourself in a Photo 149
Delete a Photo 150
Upload a Video to Facebook 150

Chapter 9: Exploring Groups, Events, and Games 153

Find Your Favorite Things on Facebook 154
Join a Facebook Group 159
Start a Facebook Group 162
Communicate with Group Members 167
Create an Event Invitation 170
Review Upcoming Events 172
Export an Event to Another Calendar 173
Have Some Fun with Games and Applications 174
Browse Facebook Apps and Games 176

Part III: And Now, It's Twitter Time 181

Chapter 10: A Beginner's Guide to Twitter..................... 183

Register with Twitter 184
Find People to Follow.. 188
Adjust Your Account Settings 194
Upload Your Avatar 197
Select a Theme for Your Profile Page... 199
Set Up Notices... 200
Know Twitter Shorthand 201

Chapter 11: Conversing on Twitter with Friends, Family, and More 203

Follow Basic Guidelines for Conversing..................................... 204
Pass Along a Chosen Tweet 206
Favorite Your Favorite Tweets 208
Search for Tweeted Topics 210
Know What to Tweet About 210

Chapter 12: Gathering Tools of the Twitter Trade 215

Search for Tweeps on WeFollow.. 216
Add Yourself to WeFollow... 221
Find Trends with Summize 222
FollowFriday, FF, and Other Hashtags 226
Connect with People.. 230
Keep Track of Hundreds, Thousands of Friends? 232
View Your Friend Lists 235

Part IV: The Rest of the Social Networking Story 239

Chapter 13: Sharing (and Grabbing) Photos, Videos, and Music 241

Give Credit When You Share 242
Make Your Links Short 245
Share Your Photos with Twitpic.. 250

Become an Online Deejay (DJ) 254

Spin Your Songs for Online Friends.. 256

Find and Share Videos on YouTube 258

Chapter 14: Giving or Taking an Opinion 263

Check Out Angie's List.. 264

Find Anything (and Its Reviews) on Amazon.................................... 265

Find Restaurants, Shopping, and Nightlife on Yelp!........................ 268

Register on Yelp to Leave Reviews 270

Leave a Review on Yelp 272

Read Between the Lines at Review Sites 274

Find Hotel Reviews on TripAdvisor 276

Add a Hotel Review on TripAdvisor 278

Find a Good Movie on Flixster 282

Leave a Comment on Flixster.. 284

Chapter 15: So You Want to Be a Blogger? 285

Answer These Questions Before You Start.. 286

Stake Your Claim in the Blogosphere.. 288

Register Your Blog.. 289

Give Your Blog a Name 291

Post Your Story with Photos 293

Set Up Your Profile 300

Index... **305**

I've been working and playing online since the mid-'80s. I started out using CompuServe from my old Kaypro II with a 300-baud modem. I'd log on to my computer in the evenings when I had some quiet time after work, after my daughter was asleep.

The online world I found through CompuServe had no fancy pages, videos, or even photos. Just phosphor-green text on a tiny screen. The early onliners didn't know any better technology, so we communicated with people by sending words across the country and across the world. We chatted with each other and joined groups to discuss our hobbies and our families.

Drawing an analogy here, there have been related social communities online for as long as there have been connected computers. Even though the kids today may think they invented the current online world, today's social media are just the 21st-century continuation of a community we've known for quite a while.

Many people who were online then (in the early '80s) are still online now. People *of a certain age* may also (after a long career) want to jump back into the family feeling of an online community. So, even though this book title says *For Seniors*, you should know I don't like that term. This book is for those with experience.

Although a persistent rumor claims that only the youngsters go online, actually online participation is growing faster in people over 50. There are more online users over 40 than under 25. Perhaps these people were so busy living their lives and bringing up their children that they didn't have extra time for themselves then — but they do now. And just as in the '60s or '70s, they don't want to be left out of anything. They want to be smack dab in the middle of the online revolution.

Unfortunately, a lot of what they encounter when they go online is unfamiliar stuff. So (naturally enough) some of the experienced, graying generation experience a feeling of trepidation when it comes to the Internet — most of all, they're a bit unsure about getting on Twitter and Facebook.

I have to say: *Why?* Participating in social media is freeing — and can bring so much into your life! You can't *not* be there!

I encourage you: Join your extended family, your children, and your friends online. By participating in social media, you'll find many of your old friends. I reconnected with my first boyfriend on Twitter, and we share family photos on Facebook. In a world where people don't chat on the phone much anymore, the online arena is the perfect place to connect.

And you will also make *new* friends. I am blessed enough to have met many of my online friends in person. The online world has given me a whole new group of people that I can call on for advice — or, better yet, go out to brunch with — in the real world.

Twitter is pretty straightforward — once you get the hang of it, you'll be tweeting like a pro in no time. But a Web site that's as complex as Facebook has many nooks and crannies that can confuse new users (and even experienced ones). Think of this book as a roadmap that can help you find your way around in the social media, getting just as much or as little as you want from the trip. Unlike an actual road map, however, you won't have to fold it back to its original shape (whew). Just close the book and come back any time you need a question answered.

About This Book

Remember those open-book tests that teachers sprang on you in high school? Well, sometimes you may feel like Facebook pop-quizzes you while you're online. Think of *Facebook & Twitter For Seniors For Dummies*, as your open-book-test cheat sheet with the answers. You don't have to memorize anything; just keep this book handy and follow along whenever you need to.

With this in mind, I've divided this book into pertinent sections to help you find your answers fast. I'll show you how to

→ Set up your computer for the ultimate online experience.

→ Learn to use online searches and tools to widen your online reach.

→ Set up a new account on Gmail to handle all your new communication.

→ Get online and register to start meeting old (and new) friends.

→ Post to your friend's Facebook Timeline and send special messages.

→ Find people you haven't heard from in years and catch up with their lives.

→ See what's going on with your children and grand-children online — and join the party.

→ Share photos and videos online.

→ Become a part of a unique community of people!

Do not reach for your glasses. To protect the privacy of the online community, the screen images (commonly called *screen shots*) that I've used in this book blur e-mail addresses on purpose. That's to protect the innocent (or not so . . . what the heck, cue the *Dragnet* theme).

Conventions Used in This Book

Anyone born before 1960 grew up in an analog age. Televisions were big, bulky affairs; the first remote controls ca-chunked each time they changed the channel (and they only had four buttons). Families woke up and went to sleep seeing a test pattern. Cameras (the good ones) were solid, heavy devices — and movie cameras whirred along with a comfortable mechanical hum. Typewriters clacked in a danceable rhythm.

Then life turned digital without anyone's permission — even without folks noticing until it happened. The comfortable mechanical sounds of everyday appliances seemed to go away. Whirring, buzzing, and beeping replaced the familiar sounds. Everything got more complex: the button count on my remote control went from four to a gazillion! It seems as if everything we use has gotten smaller. Some of those little digital cameras look so small and cheesy that I'm shocked they can take a good picture — but they do. (They take great ones!) Even the type on a page, it seems, has gotten smaller — which is why my publisher has graciously set this book in a type that will permit you to read something, glance at your computer, and look back again without having to pick your glasses off the top of your head.

Here are a few conventions to look out for as you read this book:

⟹ **Online addresses:** The online location (or address) of a Web site is called a Uniform Resource Locator (URL). These online addresses — as well as e-mail addresses — appear in a `monofont` typeface, as follows:

`www.facebook.com`

➠ **What to type:** When instructions for a task require that you type something on your keyboard, that something appears in **bold** typeface.

➠ **On-screen buttons with long labels:** When an on-screen button is labeled with a phrase instead of a single word, I put it in title case, like this: Click the Do This Silly Digital Thing Now button. That ought to head off confusion at the pass.

Foolish Assumptions

I'm thinking that you've picked up this book because you heard that the immediate world has jumped online and maybe you feel a little left out. Perhaps you already like to send text messages and think this Twitter thing might be for you? If either of these assumptions is true, this is the right book for you.

Here are some other foolish assumptions I've made about you (I'm famous for my foolish assumptions . . . you too?):

➠ You have access to a computer and the Internet (or plan to get it soon!) so you can get online and start to socialize.

➠ You have an interest in communicating with people, and you want to find out more about what you can do online — without asking your children.

➠ You want tips to help you get online without looking like a newcomer, or *newbie* (the kids call them *noobs*). I can relate. We have a lot in common.

➠ You're concerned about maintaining your privacy and staying away from shysters.

How This Book Is Organized

This book has four parts. The chapters stand on their own, meaning you can read Chapter 5 after you read Chapter 10 or skip Chapter 3 altogether. It's all up to you. If you've already dipped your toe into the online pool, you can fly ahead to get good tips on advanced tasks. Don't wait for permission from me or think that you have to read the entire book from start to finish. Feel free to go directly to the sections you're interested in. Following is a general breakdown of the book's content.

Part I: Computer and Internet Basics

Consider Part I a refresher course if you're experienced in using computers. I tell you about computer basics that give you the foundation for a good online experience. I explain the shortcuts and features in Web browsing, and show you the advantage of having an online e-mail account. You also discover some of the top social networking sites to get you talking the talk quickly.

Part II: Putting Your Face onto Facebook

If you're ready to dive into Facebook with both feet (or headfirst if you're really impetuous), check out Part II, which gives you the lowdown on everything you need to get up and running as an online denizen.

You find out how to register, share photos and videos, join groups, post messages to your friends (both privately and publically), and so much more. The world of Facebook is ever-expanding, and this part gives you all the tools you need to lead the pack. Once you learn the basics, the rest just falls into place.

Part III: And Now, It's Twitter Time

From registering to becoming a Twitter-maven, it's all here. You've got enough information to get you tweeting in no time. I show you how to meet people (which is just a little more difficult on Twitter than Facebook) and benefit from Twitter traditions — such as Follow Friday.

Part IV: The Rest of the Social Networking Story

In this part, I show you some other sites you might like to visit to share music and read (and post) online reviews of businesses, products, and services. I've included a tutorial on how to blog — and show how you can have your own blog on the Internet without it costing you a penny.

It's all so much fun. I can't wait for you to get started.

Where to Go from Here

Like everything else in the world, Twitter and Facebook have an ever-changing nature. And for Facebook — because the Web site is more complex — this is even truer. (That's annoying, isn't it?) These social networking sites are always trying to improve the user experience, but sometimes such changes can be confusing. My job is to arm you with an understanding of basic functions, so you won't be thrown by any minor course corrections on the site's part. If you hit rough waters, just look up the troublesome item in the book's index.

Most of all, don't get frustrated! Keep reviewing topics before you feel fully comfortable to take the plunge on Twitter and Facebook. Perhaps even start off with baby steps — with either site there's no need to start off with a bang. No one will notice that you're just a beginner.

A persistent piece of Internet lore quotes Albert Einstein as saying, "I never commit to memory anything that can easily be looked up in a book." But nobody seems to know exactly when he said that. No problem. You and I know that books are handy to have around when you're learning new things. I'm all about that. So is this book.

Feedback, Please

I'd love to hear from you: your successes and your comments. I'm on Twitter every day as @MarshaCollier (http://twitter.com/marshacollier). Feel free to join me on Facebook: I have my personal page, a book fan page, and a community page set up by Facebook with my biography. I love making new friends and will be glad to help you whenever I can.

Contact me at talk2marsha@coolebaytools.com or on my site, www.marshacollier.com I can't always answer each and every question you send. But do know that I promise to read each e-mail and answer when I can.

Visit my blog at http://mcollier.blogspot.com, and if you'd like to learn about eBay, check out my Web site at www.coolebay tools.com. I also wrote *eBay For Seniors For Dummies*, so if you're looking to make a little spare cash, that book will definitely simplify selling (and buying) on eBay for you.

Every Saturday from noon to 2:00 p.m. Pacific Time, I co-host the *Computer and Technology Show* on radio with Marc Cohen. You can also call in and speak to us live during the show at 877-474-3302 if we can ever help you with your computer problems. The show is also archived online at www.computerandtechnologyradio.com and on iTunes.

Welcome to the future. It's actually kind of a fun place.

Part I
Computer and Internet Basics

The 5th Wave   By Rich Tennant

"It worked, honey! I'm connected to the network!"

Getting a Computer Ready for the Internet

Chapter

1

Don't worry, I'm not going to tell you that you need really fancy equipment to get started online, but you must *have* a computer. These days, there are more choices than you can imagine for joining the online social scene. If you're in the market for a computer, you've got a few choices, which I tell you about in this chapter.

Shopping for a computer can be a dizzying experience. As a matter of fact, it's downright confusing. I suggest you go to a store and kick a few tires (or try out a few keyboards) before you make a decision. Also, recognize that your decisions about computer equipment depend on how and where you plan to use your computer. Follow my advice in this chapter to evaluate your computer use and find the right source for your equipment.

Get ready to . . .

➠ Pick Hardware to Match Your Computer Use 12

➠ Know What Hardware Options to Look For 16

➠ Shop for Your Computer of Choice 19

➠ Browse for a Browser 21

Along with your hardware of choice and an Internet connection (see Chapter 2), you need just one more item — a software program — to interact with online social sites (such as Facebook and Twitter). When you get a computer, you get an Internet browser for free. A *browser* is the software program that lets your computer talk to the Internet. It's like having your own private cyberchauffeur. In this chapter, I also tell you a little about the common browsers that are readily available.

Pick Hardware to Match Your Computer Use

1. I confess, I have a desktop, a laptop, *and* a netbook computer — and I use each one at different locations and for different reasons. You certainly don't need to have all three varieties to work with Facebook and Twitter; simply decide on which type is right for you before you buy. Think through the scenarios in this section and see which one matches your plans. Then go find the computer hardware that fits.

2. If you are one who likes to sit at a desk or table, or wants a regular place to use your computer, you'll be happy with a desktop variety. Also, if you like to have all the power of today's computing at your disposal, you'll have to get a desktop. *Desktop* computers are larger than their portable cousins, and can hold more bells and whistles.

 These days you can buy a package that combines a monitor, keyboard, and a computer module. But with all the great deals on the Internet, you may want to make these purchases separately. See the section "Shop for Your Computer of Choice" for more about where to purchase.

3. If you're looking for a computer that will allow you to sit seductively at Starbucks — looking cool — you'll have to get a laptop. Okay, how about if you just want to use Twitter or Facebook from *anywhere* in your home other than your desk (say, the kitchen counter)? The major difference between a desktop and a *laptop* (as shown in

Figure 1-1) is that everything you need is combined in one compact, lightweight package. Also, you'll be able to use your laptop (called *notebook* by some) to go online anywhere a wireless (WiFi) connection is available. WiFi readiness is built into all laptops these days.

Figure 1-1

Also consider the following if you're leaning toward getting a laptop:

• You'll find that keyboards can get progressively smaller, depending on the size of notebook you buy. So if you have big fingers, be sure to test out the notebook offerings in a store prior to buying one.

• You'll find smaller monitors on today's laptops, so they can be portable. It somewhat defeats the portability purpose when you have to lug around a 26-inch, 6-pound behemoth. Keep in mind that Web browsers allow you to easily increase the size of the text you see (more about that in the task "Browse for a Browser" later in this chapter).

I've taken my laptop out by the pool when I'm on vacation, and at home, I sometimes *tweet* (send a message on Twitter) from my garden. Portability is a wonderful thing.

4. If you're looking for extra portability and convenience, think netbook. *Netbooks* are smaller than desktops or laptops (they generally have 10-inch screens), you can stick them in a purse or shopping bag, and you can buy one for as little at $300. They are a great deal. My netbook, shown in **Figure 1-2** (nail polish is for scale), is an Asus Seashell, and it weighs a little over two pounds.

Figure 1-2

Due to size limitations, there are a few tasks that a netbook can't perform, as illustrated in **Table 1-1**.

Table 1-1   What a Laptop and a Netbook Can Do

Task	Netbook	Laptop
E-mail, chat, instant messaging	X	X
Social networking, blogging, Twitter, and Facebook	X	X
Surfing the Web	X	X
Streaming audio or video	X	X
Using word processors, spreadsheets, and small business programs	X	X
Capturing live action with a built-in Web cam	X	X
Playing games	Online Games	PC Games
Editing videos and photos	Lower resolution photos only	X
Converting music from CDs to Mp3 files		X
Seamlessly watching HD movies		X
Running complex software		X

 My laptop gets the most use, but my netbook always travels with me. But don't think that netbooks are just for traveling; they can easily fulfill your every need for using online services.

5. If you really want to Tweet or Facebook from your pocket, you can do so from any of the current smartphones. A *smartphone* is truly a mobile personal computer that fits in your hand, and you can also use it to make phone calls. Smartphones often contain mini versions of almost every piece of software you have on your laptop. When your WiFi connection is out, or if you have the need to connect from a restaurant, your smartphone can do the trick.

Popular smartphones include the iPhone, Blackberry, Android, and the Palm Pre. **Figure 1-3** shows my phone ready for action.

Figure 1-3

Know What Hardware Options to Look For

1. Before you purchase one of the different types of
equipment I outline in the previous section, think
about some of the options you need to look for on any
computing device that you plan to use for interacting
with your pals on Facebook and Twitter. Look for a
computer with a large hard drive. The more time you
spend using — and storing stuff on — your computer,
the more Blob-like your hard drive's contents become.
(Remember that 1950s horror movie, *The Blob*, where an
alien life form just grows and grows?)

A hard drive with at least 60 gigabytes (GB) of storage
space should keep your computer happy, but you can get
hard drives as big as 500 GB. You're probably going to be

storing photos and videos (yes, you will — I promise), so I suggest that you buy one with the biggest hard drive you can afford.

2. One USB port is *never* enough. These days, it seems like every peripheral device you need connects to your computer through a Universal Serial Bus (USB) connection. You may end up with an external hard drive for backup, a mouse, a printer, and a digital camera that you need to connect (so you can download pictures). **Figure** 1-4 shows a common peripheral device: a USB flash drive. Make sure that the desktop, laptop, or netbook computer you get has at *least* two USB ports (you can plug and unplug from these at will).

Figure 1-4

3. Make sure the computer's central processing unit (CPU) is fast. A *CPU* (also known as a *chip*) is your computer's brain. It should be the fastest you can afford. You can always opt for the top-of-the-line, but even a slower 900MHz (megahertz) processor *could* suffice. The popular Atom processor from Intel is in most netbook computers, and that clocks at 1.6 GHz (gigahertz). If you want lightning-fast speed (imagine a Daytona 500 race car with jet assist), you have to move up to one that boosts to at least 3.6 GHz.

4. Get a CD/DVD drive; a disc burner is standard equipment. You use the drive to load new software programs into your computer from compact discs. You can also use the CDs or DVDs for your backups. These days, all models play and record DVD movies on your computer, and most new software comes in the CD or DVD format.

5. You must have a keyboard. No keyboard, no typing. The basic keyboard is fine. They do make funky ergonomic models that are split in the middle. But if the good old standard keyboard feels comfortable to you, stick with it.

6. Multiple media-card reader. Your digital camera will no doubt have a memory card in it where it holds all the pictures you take. It's a lot easier to pop out the card and slip it into your computer than mess around with connecting cables so you can download your photos. Different cameras take different sizes of media cards, and camera manufacturers haven't really conformed to a standard yet. So it's a plus when the computer accepts multiple cards — because you'll probably get a new camera before you get a new computer.

7. You need a pointing device that moves the pointer around the computer screen; it's usually a *mouse*. Laptops and netbooks come with touchpads or trackballs designed to do the moving and give you a quick way to select options by clicking or tapping. I personally find that a mouse is a better choice.

 To save possible pain in your hands, I recommend you use an ergonomic mouse like the Contour Mouse from Contour Design (`http://ergo.contourdesign.com`). I've used one for over a decade. See **Figure 1-5**. The Contour Mouse fits your hand and is available in seven different sizes, for right and left hands. This mouse reduces or eliminates the grip force required to navigate and click traditional mice. This sculpted mouse is designed to support your hand comfortably without the need to clutch the mouse to control it.

Figure 1-5

8. When buying a monitor to go with a desktop computer, size counts! An LCD (Liquid Crystal Display) monitor that has at least a 17 inch screen can make a huge difference in your comfort level after several hours of rabid tweeting or reading your friends' Facebook posts. Anything smaller, and you could have a hard time actually seeing the words and images. The good news: Monitors have become so inexpensive that you can find a 20-inch or larger variety for about $200.

Shop for Your Computer of Choice

1. These days you can find computers at many retailers, including Office Depot, Staples, Apple Store, Sony Style, and my favorite, Costco. Try out each computer and ask questions. Every brick-and-mortar retailer these days is more than willing to show you the options they offer.

2. You can also get online and find sellers who have even better deals on new, used, or refurbished computer equipment. Some Web sites that include computers for sale are Amazon (www.amazon.com), Buy.com (www.buy.com), BestBuy.com (www.bestbuy.com), and even at Costco.com (www.costco.com).

3. If you don't feel comfortable buying a used machine (but want to save money), you may want to consider a factory-refurbished model. These are new machines that were returned to the manufacturer for one reason or another. The factory fixes them so they're nice and spiffy, and then sweetens the deal with a terrific warranty. Some companies even offer optional, extended, on-site repairs. What you're getting is a new computer at a deep discount because the machine can't be resold legally as new. Here are some things to know about refurbished computers:

- **They're rebuilt and come with warranties.** For the most part, refurbished computers are defined as returns, units with blemishes (scratches, dents, and so on), or evaluation units. The factories rebuild them to their original working condition, using new parts (or sometimes used parts that meet or exceed performance specs for new parts). They come with 60- to 90-day warranties that cover repairs and returns. Warranty information is available on the manufacturers' Web sites, so be sure to read it before you purchase a refurbished computer.

- **You can get name brands.** Major computer manufacturers such as Dell, IBM, Sony, Hewlett-Packard, and Apple provide refurbished computers. Check whether their Web site has an outlet store (**Figure 1-6** shows one example). I visit `shopping.hp.com/outlet`, `www.sonystyle.com/outlet`, and `www.dell.com/outlet`, and check the sites for closeouts and refurbished goods all the time — and I've never been burned!

Because the inventory of refurbished computers changes daily (as do the prices), there's no way of telling exactly how much money you can save by buying refurbished instead of new. I suggest that you find a new computer system you like (and can afford) in a store or a catalog, and then compare it with refurbished systems of the same brand and model.

Figure 1-6

 If you're thinking about buying from the Web or a catalog, don't forget to include the cost of shipping in the total price. Even with shipping costs, however, a refurbished computer may save you between 30% and 60%, depending on the deal you find.

Browse for a Browser

1. The two most popular *browsers* (the software programs that help you read what's on the Internet) are Firefox (available both for MAC and the PC) and Microsoft Internet Explorer. (They are to browsers what Coca-Cola and Pepsi are to the cola wars.) Both programs are powerful and user-friendly. Type the address (also known as the *URL*, for *Uniform Resource Locator*) of the Web site you want to visit, and boom, you're there. For example, to get to Twitter's home page, type **www.twitter.com** in the browser's address box and press Enter. (It's sort of a low-tech version of "Beam me up, Scotty!" — and almost as fast.)

According to recent statistics, the most popular browsers are Internet Explorer, Firefox, Chrome, and Safari. **Figures 1-7** and **1-8** show you the first two browsers and how they show pages in the same way. (Sit, browser! Now shake! *Good* browser!) The one you choose is a matter of preference — I use them both!

A Web page in Firefox

Figure 1-7

The same page in Internet Explorer

Figure 1-8

2. You can get Microsoft Internet Explorer and Firefox for free. To find out more information (or to make sure you're using the most up-to-date version of the software), go to:

- www.microsoft.com for Microsoft Internet Explorer

- www.mozilla.com/firefox for Firefox

3. If you've ever wondered what all those buttons and drop-down lists at the top of your browser do, now's the time to check it out. At the top of almost all Microsoft-enabled programs are standard drop-down menus that invoke

various functions. (If they don't appear on your version, press the Alt key.) Who'd ever think you'd need to use menus, given all the colorful icons that Internet Explorer provides? Well, the drop-down menus give you more in-depth access to what the program can do. **Table 1-2** and **Table 1-3** give you an overview of the various tasks you can perform from these menus.

Table 1-2	Internet Explorer Menus
Menu	*What You Can Do*
File	Open, print, save, and send HTML Web pages
Edit	Select, cut, copy, paste, and find text on the currently displayed page
View	Change the way Explorer displays Internet pages
Favorites	Save your favorite pages in the Favorites file
Tools	Enable pop-up blockers, add filters, and clear your machine's history of the Web sites you've visited
Help	Find help

Table 1-3	Firefox Menus
Menu	*What You Can Do*
File	Open, print, save, and send HTML Web pages
Edit	Select, cut, copy, paste, and find text on the currently displayed page
View	Change the way Firefox displays Internet pages
History	See and navigate back and forth among the sites visited in your current session
Bookmarks	Bookmark a page or access your saved bookmarks (same as "favorites" in Internet Explorer)
Tools	Enable features, install add-on programs, clear Private Data, and set browser options
Help	Find help

4. As a *graphical interface,* Internet Explorer also presents you with colorful icons that allow you to invoke programs or tasks with a click of the mouse. You find these icons on the toolbars at the top of your browser window (refer to **Figure 1-8**).

5. If you want to add speed to your browsing and cut down your desk time, get comfy with using keyboard and mouse shortcuts. I'm all about using keystrokes instead of always pointing and clicking! I also love the controls available on my mouse. **Table 1-4** and **Table 1-5** give you a list of all the shortcuts I could find. You'll see that Internet Explorer and Firefox share some shortcuts.

Table 1-4	Internet Explorer Shortcuts
Press This	*Explorer Will*
F1	Open a help window
Ctrl and F	Open the Search box so you can perform a search for a specific word on the current page
F4	Open your URL list so you can click back to a site that you just visited
F5	Refresh the current page
F11	Display full screen, reducing the number of icons and amount of other stuff displayed
Esc	Stop loading the current page
Home	Go back to the top of the Web page
End	Jump to the bottom of the current page
Backspace	Go back to the last Web page you viewed
Ctrl and + (plus sign); Ctrl and – (minus sign)	Enlarge or reduce the text on the screen
Ctrl and D	Add the current page to your Favorites list. (Don't forget to organize this list once in a while!)

Table 1-5	Firefox Shortcuts
Press This	*Firefox Will*
Backspace	Go to the previous page you've viewed
Ctrl and O	Open a window to open files from your computer
Ctrl and U	View Page source (to study HTML)
F11	Display full-screen, reducing the amount of icons and stuff displayed
Esc	Stop loading the current page
Ctrl and P	Print the page
Ctrl and S	Save the current page to a file on your computer
Ctrl and + (plus sign) or Ctrl and – (minus sign)	Enlarge or reduce the text on the screen
Ctrl and F	Find a word on the current Web page

Hooking Up to the Internet

*Y*ou're settled on your computer, and you're ready to get started with social connections on the Web. Before you start checking out sites such as Facebook and Twitter, you need *access* to the Internet. (Details, details . . . .) The way to access the Internet is through an *Internet service provider*, or ISP, such as Earthlink, AT&T, or RoadRunner. If you don't already belong to one of these, don't worry; joining is easy, as I describe in this chapter.

ISPs offer two basic types of connections: dial-up (slower, but less expensive) and broadband (faster and pricier). In this chapter, I fill you in on some details to help you decide what's right for you. Also, I tell you about the wired or wireless networking methods that complete the setup you need for easy access to Facebook and Twitter.

Over the years, I have written what seems like volumes of tips to keep people safe online. But I know this book won't have to give you all the whys and wherefores — you've been around the block (as have I) — so I give you just a few easy-to-follow rules for staying safe during your online social interactions.

Chapter 2

Get ready to . . .

➠ Select an Internet Service Provider 28

➠ Set Up a Dial-Up Connection 31

➠ Choose a Broadband Network Option 32

➠ Connect a Powerline Network 34

➠ Connect a Wireless Network 36

➠ Remember These Rules to Stay Safe Online 41

Select an Internet Service Provider

1. If you plan to join a telephone dial-up ISP (because dial-up requires no additional equipment or connections in most — usually older — computers), just load the freebie software that comes with a computer and follow the registration steps that appear on your computer screen. (Also see the next section in this chapter.) A new computer may come with a free trial of America Online (AOL) or some other ISP. Before you put up your credit card, use your free trial to scout the Web for the best deals on getting hooked up to the Internet.

 When you go to a computer store or buy a computer, you're hit with all kinds of free trial offers that beg you to "Sign up now, first month free!" You can find free introductory deals everywhere! If you're new to the Internet and not sure which ISP to go with, your best bet may be to start with NetZero. NetZero has been around for years, and offers accelerated speeds on their dial-up connections.

2. If you have a need for speed, you may want to look into getting a broadband connection. The quality of the different types of broadband (DSL and cable) can vary greatly from area to area and even from street to street. Before you decide what kind of broadband connection you want, use your local library or friend's computer and go to the following Web site, shown in **Figure 2-1**:

www.broadbandreports.com

Type your ZIP code, press Enter, and read the reports for other users in your area. You can e-mail, post questions, and get all the information you need to decide what kind of high-speed connection will work best for you.

Type your ZIP code here.

Figure 2-1

3. If you decide that your time is worth a bit more than an increase in ISP cost, broadband (high-speed) connections can save you bunches of time when you're flying through Facebook photos. Here's the skinny on the different types:

- *DSL:* Short for *Digital Subscriber Line.* For as little as $19.95 a month, you can get rid of your pokey, analog dial-up connection and always be connected to the Internet. A DSL line can move data as fast as 6 MB per second — that's six *million* bits per second, or 140 times as fast as a 56K modem. At that speed, a DSL connection can greatly enhance your interaction with Facebook and Twitter, as well as any other Internet experience. For more information about what DSL is and how to get it, visit http://www.dslreports.com.

• *Cable:* An Internet cable connection is a reliable method for Internet access if you have digital cable TV. Your Internet connection runs through your television cable to a modem, and is regulated by your cable TV provider. With the advent of digital cable, this reliable and speedy Internet connection is an excellent alternative. (See my speed report from my wireless network in **Figure 2-2**.) Most cable accounts include several e-mail addresses for everyone in your family.

Figure 2-2

4. You have one more type of Internet connection to consider: public WiFi. *WiFi* stands for Wireless Fidelity, which describes a particular (and common) wireless technology for local networking without wires (that is, via a radio frequency). Believe it or not, there are lots of public places where you can find wireless Internet access that's free or has a very low fee. That's right — depending on the computer system you choose (see Chapter 1) and how much time you intend to spend online, you may not need an ISP of your own. All you need is a portable computer — netbook or laptop — that has a wireless connection (and all the new ones do these days).

To find free WiFi when you want to go portable, find
your nearest coffee house and ask whether they have a
free WiFi connection. If so, get connected and visit
www.wififreespot.com. At this site, as shown in
Figure 2-3, you can look up restaurant, hotel, and retail
chains that offer WiFi in all their locations along with a
state-by-state listing of small businesses and other
locations that offer free WiFi.

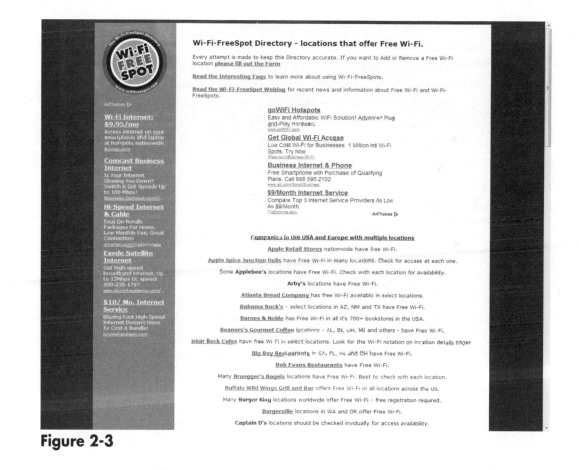

Figure 2-3

Set Up a Dial-Up Connection

1. If you want to set up a dial-up connection, follow these
simple steps. Run the free dial-up software that comes on
your computer. It will prompt you through a registration
process, so be sure to fill in all the blanks.

2. When prompted, get a phone cable and plug it into your computer's modem card and into a phone jack on the wall nearby.

3. Following the software instructions, you should merely need to wait until you hear some strange sounds coming from your computer (connecting noise) and your computer will connect with the service.

 Even if you start out with a standard dial-up connection, I honestly don't expect you to stay with it for too long. Once you get the hang of running from profile to profile on Facebook or tweeting to your heart's content on Twitter, you're going to want some serious speed. Don't worry; the next section in this chapter tells you how to hook up to broadband and get the speed you need.

Choose a Broadband Network Option

1. When you set up your Internet connection with anything other than a direct dial-up connection to your computer, you're actually setting up the beginnings of a home network. By networking your home, you can save time — not to mention gain convenience — because you add the flexibility of taking your laptop into different rooms or locations. You can also tweet from out by your pool (or in your backyard) during summer!

 A *network* is a way to connect computers so they can communicate with each other as if they were one giant computer with different terminals. The best part of this idea is that a network lets several computers share a high-speed (broadband) Internet connection — and you can share printers and gaming devices as well. When you set up a computer network, your home can become a WiFi hotspot!

2. You have a choice of three types of home networks:
Ethernet, powerline, and wireless. See **Table 2-1** for a
quick rundown of some pros and cons of each.

Table 2-1	Network Pros and Cons	
Network type	**Pros**	**Cons**
Ethernet	Fast, cheap, and easy to set up	Everything must be wired together, cables run everywhere
Powerline	Fast, because your home is prewired with electrical outlets	Electrical interference may degrade signal
Wireless network	Fast, no ugly cables to deal with	More expensive, possible interference from electrical devices

While you make a decision about the type of network
you want to use, consider the following points:

- The wireless network is currently the hot ticket and is
  becoming a standard. If you have a laptop and a high-
  speed connection, you deserve to have WiFi in your home.
  Any day now, you'll want to stream video from your notebook to your television. WiFi can do that and more!

- With broadband over powerline networking, you get
  high-speed Internet directly into your home electrical
  system. Just plug in your powerline boxes (more on
  that later) and you're up and running!

3. Regardless of the type of network you choose, all networks need the following two devices:

- **Router:** A router allows you to share a single Internet
  connection among multiple devices. A router does
  exactly what its name says: It routes signals and data
  to and from the different devices on your network. If
  you have one computer, the router can act as a firewall or even as a network device, allowing you to have
  a wireless printer (I have one — it's great) and a connection for a gaming device.

You can connect as many computers, printers, or game systems (Wii, Xbox, or PS3 — yours or the kids') as you like, and reach the Internet from anywhere in your home. You can even hook up your laptop from the bedroom if you don't feel like getting out of bed.

- **Modem:** You need a broadband modem for a high-speed Internet connection, and you get one from your cable or phone company. To install, plug the modem into an outlet with cable (just like your TV) or into a phone jack with the phone line for DSL. The modem connects to your router with a short length of Ethernet cable.

 If you have broadband, and have more than one computer, you don't need to have a main computer turned on to access the connection from anywhere in the house.

Connect a Powerline Network

1. An ingenious invention, a powerline network uses your existing home power lines to carry your network and your high-speed Internet connection. You access the network by plugging a powerline adapter from your computer into an electrical outlet in the wall. Powerline networks have been around for a while and are in their second round of technological advances.

2. When deciding what kind of network to set up, consider these benefits of a nifty little powerline system:

- **It's inexpensive.** The requisite powerline magic box costs around $40, but you'll need one for each computer.

- **It's fast, as fast or faster than other network connections.** You could stream DVD movies from one room to another.

- **The networking connection is made through your existing electrical wiring.** It doesn't consume extra electricity.

- **Installation is easy.** Just plug a cable into your computer, and connect the cable to the powerline adapter. Plug the powerline adapter into the wall outlet.

3. To set up a powerline network, you need the following items in addition to a router and modem (which you need for any network):

- **Electrical outlets:** I'll bet you have more than one in each room.

- **An Ethernet connection on each computer:** All new computers come with an Ethernet outlet.

- **Powerline Ethernet bridge for each computer:** You plug an Ethernet cable from your computer into the powerline Ethernet bridge, a small box about the size of a pack of cigarettes that plugs into any two- or three-prong electrical outlet. See Figure 2-4.

Figure 2-4
Photo courtesy of Netgear

4. Hooking up a powerline network is so easy that it's a bit disappointing — you'll wonder why it isn't more complicated. If you have a high-speed Internet connection, you received a modem when you signed up. Because it's not common to connect the modem directly to your computer (a router does the network routing for you), you may already have a router.

The integration works like this:

1. *The high-speed connection comes in through your DSL or cable line.*

2. *The cable (or DSL) line plugs into your modem.*

3. *An Ethernet cable goes from your modem into a router.*

4. *One "out" Ethernet cable connection from the router goes to a local computer.*

5. *Another "out" Ethernet cable goes to the powerline adapter.*

6. *The powerline box plugs into a convenient wall outlet.*

5. When you want to connect the computers in other rooms to the network, just plug in a magic powerline box. **Figure 2-5** shows you the basic setup for (say) a home office. Other rooms need only a powerline adapter that you hook up to a computer, game device, and so on, running an Ethernet cable from the adapter to the device's network card.

Connect a Wireless Network

1. Wireless networking (also known as WiFi) is the hot technology for all kinds of networks. It's an impressive system, with no cables or connectors to bog you down. You're probably more familiar with wireless technology than you may think at first. If you've ever used a wireless telephone at home, you've used a technology similar to a wireless network. Most home wireless phones transmit on the radio frequency band of 2.4GHz (gigahertz) and offer an option to choose from several channels automatically to give you the best connection.

Figure 2-5
Figure courtesy of Netgear

 Here's an FYI on all those signals running around and about your house. AM radio broadcasts from 53KHz (kilohertz) to 1.7MHz (megahertz), and FM radio, television, cell phones, GPS, and the space station broadcast in megahertz. One gigahertz (GHz) is a thousand kilohertz, so it won't be interfering with other radio frequency signals.

2. The two prevalent forms of wireless networks also work on the 2.4GHz band; you'll need to preset the channel when you set up the system. There are basically four types of wireless formats, and the newer types are usually *backward-compatible* (that means the newer types work well with the older types). Be sure to check out the various computers, routers, and so on that you want to connect together in your network; in particular, find out which wireless format(s) they use. Those formats are

➡ **802.11a:** This wireless format works really well; fast with good connectivity. It's used when you have to serve up a wireless connection to a large group of people, such as in a convention center or a dormitory. This isn't something you'll use at home.

➡ **802.11b:** My old laptop has a built-in 802.11b connector, so I can connect to the ever popular WiFi hotspots in Starbucks and airports. The b version is slower than the newer versions (mentioned later in this list) and can transfer data at only 11 Mbps (11 megabits of data per second).

➡ **802.11g:** This is the next incarnation of WiFi that uses the 2.4GHz band; its nickname is "the g band." It speeds data to a possible 54 Mbps, and is backward-compatible with 802.11b service. Many older WiFi networks and gaming devices work on the g band.

➡ **802.11n:** This mode — the newest — builds on the previous standards by adding multiple-input multiple-output (MIMO) technology. MIMO uses multiple antennas (usually built into the router) to carry more information than previously possible with a single antenna. It uses the 5GHz band (an improvement on the old 2.4GHz band). It also increases speed through connection to 100 Mbps.

For maximum speed, your entire network needs to be an 802.11n, 5GHz network. In my house, my 802.11n network doesn't work at full speed because I have existing laptops on 802.11b/g. I'll continue with a mixed 802.11b/g/n network until I replace all my laptops with 802.11n. And until I do that, my system won't run at the top advertised speeds.

3. Before you start worrying about sending your data over the airwaves, you'll be glad to know that wireless networks are protected by their own brand of security.

- **WEP (Wired Equivalent Privacy):** This original technology led the way in home WiFi security. WEP encrypts your wireless transmissions and prevents others from getting into your network. Sadly, it got so that a high school kid could crack this system, so now home WiFi users have WPA (and even WPA-2) instead. For more about those, read on.

- **WPA (WiFi Protected Access)** utilizes a *pre-shared key* (PSK) mode, where every user on the network is given the same passphrase. In the PSK mode, security depends on the strength and secrecy of the pass-phrase. So to link your laptop or desktop to a wireless network with WPA encryption, you need to find out the predetermined passphrase. Just enter it during setup on every computer that uses the network, and you should be good to go.

 Most WiFi hotspots you come across may not have any encryption, and some may be free for all to use. Just be aware that some miscreants drive through neighborhoods with a WiFi scanner looking for open wireless networks. These war-driving scammers then attempt to connect to an unprotected network to hack into personal information. Be sure to set your security settings to protect your network.

4. With a wireless network, you have to hook your computer (a laptop works best) to a wireless router to perform some beginning setup tasks such as choosing your channel and setting up your WPA passphrase. When you complete the setup and turn on your wireless router, you have created a WiFi hotspot in your home or office. Typically, your new hotspot will provide coverage for at *least* 100 feet in all directions, although walls and floors cut down on the range. Even so, you should get good coverage throughout a typical home. For a large home, you can buy signal boosters to increase the range of your hotspot.

5. The following steps, although simplified, outline the process for how you configure your wireless network. **Figure** 2-6 shows a wireless network diagram from Netgear.

Xbox 350

Notebook PC with
802.11b Wireless
PC Card

Desktop PC with
802.11g Wireless
USB Adapter

Internet

802.11g Wireless
Access Point

Cable/DSL
Modem

Firewall
Router

Notebook PC with
802.11n Wireless
PC Card

Figure 2-6
Figure courtesy of Netgear.

1. *Connect an Ethernet cable from your laptop to your router.*

2. *The setup program may run automatically (or the documentation that came with your router will tell you how to invoke it). Set your security protocol and passphrase.*

3. *Follow router instructions as to whether you need to reboot the router.*

4. *Run a cable from your DSL or cable jack to your modem.*

5. *Connect an Ethernet cable from your modem to your router.*

6. *Type in the passphrase to all computers on the network, one at a time.*

Remember These Rules to Stay Safe Online

1. Don't click links you receive in e-mail messages. Even if you get an e-mail message from someone you know, don't click any links. There's no way to know for sure that their account hasn't been hacked and you're being directed to a site that can do you serious damage. Here are specific examples of e-mail messages with links that you might receive:

- **Phishing e-mails:** These e-mails purport to be from your bank, your investment broker, or even your insurance company. They ask you to click a link and when you do, you arrive on a page where you have to log in. *Do not log in* (if you've gone this far). Bad-deed doers can replicate a Web page to look very official, and what they really want is your log-in information — in particular your passwords, account information, or Social Security Number.

- **E-mails that you think are from friends:** You may get a link in an e-mail message that you think is from a friend. Don't click it unless you are sure! Sometimes these links take you to a Web site where you can get a

Trojan (a sneaky program that gives a hacker remote access to your computer), a virus (when unknowingly downloaded, replicates itself to wreck havoc on your programs or data), a worm (a variant of a virus that replicates itself transparently until it takes over all your computer's memory and possibly your hard drive), or heaven knows what. Stay safe.

- **E-mails from your bank or someone that you do business with:** Instead of clicking a link in the e-mail, go to the bank or business Web site by typing the Web address in your browser address bar as you usually do. If the bank or business has some sort of special message for you, it will show up when you sign in to your account. Most times, you will not receive an e-mail link unless you sign up with the business for automatic payments or notices.

2. Stay safe with friends. You'll find that you will have more "friends" on Twitter because Twitter is a bit more impersonal. The fun of Twitter is being able to hear from many people from different places. Also, your Twitter bio is only a sentence long and it doesn't (or at least shouldn't) give much away about you.

 Facebook's info page does show a lot of information. You might not want everyone on your friend list to be able to see everything — perhaps only your closest friends. Use Facebook's security controls (see Chapter 6) to set controls for who can see what when they visit your Facebook pages.

3. Don't give away too much information. Don't give away any bit of information that makes you feel uncomfortable. Be careful who you trust online with your home address and other contact information. *And never give away your Social Security Number!* I don't want to scare you, but someone with just a few bits of information about you can get a lot more data than you can imagine. The Internet has plenty of sites (for example, Google maps) that will even show people a photo of your house. Always be cautious.

All About E-Mail

Chapter 3

1 know, I know, you've got sending and receiving e-mail down. But did you know there's a bit more to it? You can not only use e-mail to send messages, but you can also subscribe to news lists and feeds on the Internet. And in fact, Facebook and Twitter use your e-mail account to send you notifications of activity on your (and your friends') pages, private messages, and more. You'll be surprised when your e-mail becomes your pipeline to the news your friends post on the sites. Let's get into the full picture now!

Know that your e-mail address consists of two parts. The part before the @ sign is the local part (so the server knows who to send the e-mail to). After the @ sign is the *domain address* — which tells the domain name system which mail transfer agent accepts mail for that domain.

Every Web site has a URL (its address online), and every e-mail address has a domain component. When requests for Web pages or e-mails are launched into the ethers of the Web, the routing system needs to know where they should be sent. So if you're using the e-mail address your Internet service provider (ISP) assigned you, the e-mail is sent to your user ID (your name) @ your ISP domain — literally your address on the Web.

Get ready to . . .

➠ Check Out Places to Get Your E-Mail Service 44

➠ Meet the Big Three Web-Based E-Mail Providers 46

➠ Pick a Pick-Proof Password ... 51

➠ Sign Up for a Gmail Account 52

➠ Add Your Contacts 57

➠ Compose and Send an E-mail 59

Then the mail transfer agent (MTA, a type of software) uses your online name and address to transfer electronic mail messages from one computer to another.

Also know that your e-mail address (the local part) can use any name you want, as long as someone else at the domain isn't using it. It's usually best to have at least one address with your real name for public and official use. You might want to add a second (or third, fourth, or fifth) address with different *noms de plume* for family members, friends, and specific projects. For example, I have the following names on different services:

mcollier1	eBay4Dummies
Marsha.Collier	eBayGal
Talk2Marsha	Cre8ive

There may be six different names, and all are accessible online, but they all download daily into Outlook, my e-mail program on my PC.

In this chapter, I tell you about where you can get e-mail service and take you through the basics of signing up and using Gmail, the free e-mail service from Google. Having a Gmail account is not only cool, but it's very convenient. You might prefer to give out this anonymous e-mail address to online sites for privacy reasons. It's just an extra (*and free*) convenience. Check out this chapter for more of the benefits.

Check Out Places to Get Your E-Mail Service

1. You can start your search for an e-mail account with your Internet service provider (ISP). When you signed up for your Internet service, you were probably allotted up to five e-mail accounts for different members of your family. Your ISP also assigned you a user name when you signed up. My ISP gave me my user name, but I wasn't aware that it would be the name in my e-mail address, too. (Seriously, *mcollier1* doesn't have much of a ring to it.)

Your ISP will have a Web interface where you can check your e-mail online, but it's far more efficient to use a software program on your computer for *all* your e-mail.

2. Understand that the e-mail account from your ISP has pluses and minuses, as follows:

- **Minus:** You may change Internet service providers in the future. Hence, if you're using the ISP e-mail address as your own, you'll have to change it. This will force you to contact everyone who has that e-mail address to change it in their records. I've been with my ISP for over seven years; the thought of having to send a change of address to *every single one* of my contacts is, well, loathsome.

- **Plus:** Your ISP is going to be a lot more helpful when you have a problem or a question than the Web-based free services I mention in the next step. Service providers are invested in keeping you as a paying customer. They have a customer-support staff that you can contact with problems.

3. You can also consider using a Web-based e-mail service. More and more people have found Internet-based e-mail accounts the convenient way to go. They can access these accounts online from any computer, anytime day or night. And these services are offered at no charge.

 Notice that (in the preceding step) I didn't say Web-based e-mail accounts were *free*. Although the providers don't ask for money, they do expose you to ads while you go through your e-mail. Most services have settings that allow you to download your e-mails to your home e-mail program and to your smartphone.

4. The benefits of having a Web-based e-mail address is that you can change your home ISP anytime you wish, and you won't have to notify hundreds (perhaps thousands) of connections to give your new e-mail address. In the next section, I give you an overview of the leaders in the online e-mail arena who are jockeying for your business.

Meet the Big Three Web-Based E-Mail Providers

1. Yahoo! Mail from industry veteran Yahoo! (founded in 1994, which is ancient by Internet standards) has been ratcheting up its offerings. The home page for your e-mail is a mélange of news tips, weather reports, trendy topics from the Internet, an editable calendar, ads (of course), and (finally) your e-mail boxes, as shown in **Figure 3-1**. It's a very popular service with the following features:

   • **Unlimited e-mail storage.** This means you can keep your e-mails on Yahoo forever. (I'm not sure why you'd want to keep all your mail around, but diff'rent strokes . . . .)

   • **Huge file attachments.** If you want to attach videos or other large files to your e-mails, it's easy on Yahoo! Many servers limit the size of the files you can send through e-mail. Yahoo! limits attachment size to a 25MB (megabyte) maximum.

   • **Thumbnails of images.** You may want to attach pictures to e-mails you send to your friends and family. Here you can rotate the image (ever have any photos come out sideways?) and get thumbnail-size reductions of your pictures.

   • **Yahoo! Messenger.** If you're familiar with the old AIM (AOL Instant Messenger) feature, you'll be right at home with the similar online-chat service that Yahoo! offers. You can talk to contacts in chat format who have accounts in the Yahoo service — either from the Yahoo! Web site or from a smartphone.

• **Robust Help area.** Notice the Help link in the upper-right corner of the screen. Click it to be transported to a simple-to-understand tutorial and help area.

 To access Yahoo Mail, go to `http://mail.yahoo.com`.

 The major drawback of Yahoo! Mail is that if you want to download your e-mail to your personal computer, you have to upgrade to the Plus service. Plus service costs $19.99 a year, but also does away with ads on your page.

Check, compose, and search e-mail.

Find top stories.

Read your e-mail messages.

Share your status.

Find help.

Get updates from friends and family.

Figure 3-1

2. Microsoft Hotmail is another popular online e-mail service. Hotmail lives online under the Microsoft Live umbrella. You can sign in at `http://home.live.com`, where you have a landing page for any other Live services you might use (as shown in **Figure 3-2**). You can also access Hotmail directly at `www.hotmail.com`.

 First off, you need to know that the service is only run by Microsoft; they don't fuss over what kind of computer you use. You can use either a Mac or a Windows PC and still avail yourself of Hotmail. You may know of people who have `msn.com` e-mail domains, which are also served up by the Hotmail servers.

Figure 3-2

Here are the special features of the no-cost Hotmail service:

- **5 GB storage space to start.** That's gigabytes — 1,024 megabytes *times five*! Not unlimited, but certainly more than you'll probably need to use.

- **Instant Messenger service for all Hotmail accounts.** All online mail services offer IM to their subscribers.

- **Integration with Outlook and Outlook Express** for e-mail and calendar, using the Outlook Hotmail Connector tool.

- **25 GB of online storage space for photos or documents in the SkyDrive function.** You can set the pictures and documents you store here to be private or to be shared. It's a very handy (and free) way to back up documents and pictures.

- **Import from other online e-mail services.** With an easy tool, you can import other online e-mail services into your Hotmail home page.

 If you want to upgrade — so you don't see ads, and get 10GB of storage — you can sign up for Hotmail Plus for $19.95 a year.

3. Google Mail (Gmail) — the newcomer begun in 2004 as an invitation only test — has surpassed Yahoo! Mail (the longest-running free e-mail service) in popularity. Your Google home page has a bar at the top where you can easily access any of Google's other free services. What makes Gmail popular is the array of features:

  - **10GB of storage and growing.** Google's founders say no one will ever run out of storage space. (*Ever?* Hmmm . . . we'll see.)

  - **Google Chat, which is the Google instant message service.** Unlike the other free online mail services, you can also log into the more popular AIM on your Google mail page. You also have the option of using your Webcam to have a live video chat with one of your contacts.

- **SMS (Short Message Service), or text messages, which you can send to any phone through Gmail e-mails.** All you need to know is the phone number and you can enable SMS messaging in your settings.

- **A great spam filter.** *Spam* is the name for advertising e-mail that is sent to you unsolicited by unscrupulous vendors to try to sell you goods or even to defraud you. Gmail smartly places spam in your Spam folder for you to review and delete at will. It's scathingly good at its job, check **Figure 3-3** to see all the e-mail that's been (thankfully) yanked from my Inbox.

- **Google Calendar,** an online calendar that is automatically yours when you have a Gmail account. You can opt to share your calendar with someone, or keep it private. And you see a Calendar window on your mail page. If you have a smartphone, you can view — and interactively update — your calendar from your phone.

- **Connectivity features, such as instant synchronizing (sync) with smartphones and connecting with the e-mail program on your computer.** Gmail sends your e-mail to your desktop and keeps a copy on the Gmail server until you choose to delete it. The sync function on smartphones works interactively with your phone. (When you delete an e-mail from your phone, the e-mail disappears from your screen and goes into your trash on your Gmail Web page; you can always retrieve it if you've deleted it in error.)

All that said, Gmail is currently the most popular and flexible free e-mail service. In a later section, I show how to set up a Gmail account.

Click to delete all spam.

Figure 3-3

Pick a Pick-Proof Password

When you set up an e-mail account — or any account — on the Internet, you will have to set a *password*, which is the keyword you type in to confirm your sign-in along with your user ID. Passwords are not only used in e-mail, but also on almost every Web site you become a member of. If you have a strong password, hackers will pass by your account and attempt to hack an easier target.

Picking a good password is not as thought-free — but *is* twice as important — as it may seem. Whoever has your password can (in effect) *be you* anywhere on the Web — posting comments, sending spam e-mail messages, and leaving dangerous messages (which can range from pranks to scams or worse) for others to see. Basically, such an impostor can ruin your online reputation — and possibly cause you serious financial grief.

With any online password, you should follow these common-sense rules to protect your privacy:

➡ Don't pick anything too obvious, such as your birthday, your first name, your address, or (never, never!) your Social Security number. (*Hint:* If it's too easy to remember, it's probably too easy to crack.)

➡ Make things tough on the bad guys — combine numbers and letters and create nonsensical words. Use upper *and* lower cases.

➡ Don't give out your password to *anyone* — it's like giving away the keys to the front door of your house.

➡ If you even suspect someone has your password, immediately change it.

➡ Change your password every few months just to be on the safe side. Maybe rotate a group of passwords over the various accounts you use?

Sign Up for a Gmail Account

1. I like Gmail above the other online e-mail service providers because it has great features and is easy to use. So start here to set up a Gmail account. Open your Web browser and type this URL in the address line:

```
http://mail.google.com
```

You'll see a page that looks like **Figure 3-4**. Read the information on the page and then click the New Features link near the center of the screen. Should there be any updates you need to know about, the latest news will be on this page.

Click here to sign up for Gmail.

Figure 3-4

2. In the upper-right part of your screen, see the box that
reads: *New to Gmail? Create an Account?* Yep, that's the
one, click the Create an Account button and get ready for
the magic to happen. By getting your own Gmail
account, you get access to Google's world of magic Web
tools, such as Google calendar (an interactive online calendar you can share with your family), free Blogger blogs
(more on that in Chapter 15), and Google Docs (a suite
of free online programs very similar to Microsoft Office).

3. The resulting Get Started with Gmail page (see **Figure** 3-5) is where you type in your information:

Fill in information as prompted.

Figure 3-5

- **Your name.** First and Last.

- **Desired Login Name.** Fill in what you want to become your local address and name at the Gmail domain. In **Figure 3-5**, I selected marshaismyfavorite-author as my sample name. My e-mail address will be `marshaismyfavoriteauthor@gmail.com`.

After you type in your desired name, Gmail automatically lets you know if the name is available. If it isn't, Google will make suggestions that you probably won't like. Put on your thinking cap and come up with a good login name. This name will be with you for a long time; there's no changing it later.

- **Choose a Password.** Refer to the preceding section and type your password in the box; make sure it's at least eight characters long. You'll notice (as you're typing) that Google tells you whether your selected password is Weak or Strong. Go Strong! Also, type in your password again — carefully! — to confirm it where prompted.

- **Birthday.** Google wants your birth date. Use the dropdown menu to select your birth month and fill in the date and year.

 It's okay to fib about your age, but be sure you remember the date you give Google. Should you ever forget your password, or if your account gets messed up in some way, you're going to have to supply this information. If you can't remember it, you're out of luck.

- **Gender.** Male or female? Google also provides an Other option for all the others in the world.

- **Mobile Phone.** Adding your mobile phone number here puts it on record with Google and offers the opportunity for them to send security notices or password reset instructions to your phone if they're ever needed.

- **Your current e-mail address.** Type in your ISP e-mail address so that Google can send you an e-mail message to authenticate you.

- **Word verification.** You'll see a bunch of semi-legible letters in a box. (They're called *Captcha* codes.) Try to read them — and if you can make them out, type them in as prompted. If you're wrong, the page refreshes and you get a new set of letters. (I had to do this three times until I got it right.)

- **Location.** The United States is filled into this box by default. If that's where you are, fine. If not, type in your country.

- **Stay Signed In.** Click this check box to put a check mark in it, and each time you return to your Gmail page (from this computer and browser), you won't always have to type in your password.

- **Security Question.** Select a security question from the drop-down menu — or write your own. Type in the answer in the box below this option.

 Never use your mother's maiden name as a security question on the Web. That information should be between you and your bank.

- **Terms of Service.** Here Google outlines its Terms of Service (TOS). Any Web site you sign up with has them. Read the TOS and print them if you'd like, but if you don't agree to them, you can't have a Gmail account.

- **Personalization Option.** You may see a box asking if Google can use your account to personalize content and ads on other sites. Google, as you may know, is a big business, but one of their biggest money makers is delivering ads all over the Internet. Check this if you want Google to scan your e-mail box to identify things that might interest you and deliver ads that match those interests. Deselect if you'd prefer they keep out of your business.

Click the Next Step button. The next page allows you to add a photo to your account. Follow the instructions to upload a pic if you want that extra level of personalization. If you're fine being an anonymous blue silhouette, click Next Step again. You're given the option to Continue on to Gmail and your new e-mail account.

4. The next page? It's your Gmail home page!

Add Your Contacts

1. When you first arrive at your Gmail page, take a deep breath and look around before you start to click anything. **Figure 3-6** shows you some of the important points to take in. Get familiar with the page; there's a lot to look at. You'll notice that the fine folks at Google have sent you some introductory e-mails. So why not start there?

2. One of the e-mails you have received has instructions on how to import your contacts. Move your cursor over the e-mail list. Your cursor turns into a small hand with a pointing finger. Click your mouse once and the e-mail opens!

3. You can import your contacts and existing mail from Yahoo!, Hotmail, AOL, and your ISP accounts. If you indicate that it's okay to do so, Gmail will continue to import your mail from the other servers for the next 30 days. For now, I suggest that you just close the e-mail by clicking the Back to Inbox link on the top left of the e-mail. You may just want to input your contacts manually.

4. When you're back at the Inbox, look at the drop-down menu on the upper-left side marked Gmail. Click that menu and a box opens with options to go to the Gmail, Contacts, or Tasks screen. Click Contacts from that menu, then click New Contacts on the new screen and prepare to add a contact. Your Add Contact page appears, as shown in **Figure 3-7**.

Click here to access your Inbox.

Click here to compose an e-mail.

Messages from the Gmail Team.

Click here to sign out.

Figure 3-6

5. Fill in your contact's information on the new screen. You can add the name, e-mail address, phone, address, birthday, Web site (if the person has one), and any notes you want to make. When that's done, click Add to complete other fields that don't show up on the main screen. Gmail automatically saves the info as you complete the fields and adds the contact to your list.

Figure 3-7

6. Select the contact's name from your contact list at any
time to make changes or to add information to the contact. Return to your Inbox by clicking the Contacts drop-
down menu in the upper left and selecting Inbox.

Compose and Send an E-mail

1. If you're following along, then you're probably about to
send your first Gmail e-mail. Click the link that says
Compose (at the upper left of the screen), as shown in
Figure 3-8.

2. The e-mail form opens. In the To box, type in the name of
one of your contacts or type in someone's e-mail address.

Fill in a recipient, subject, and message.

Figure 3-8

3. Type the subject of the e-mail in the Subject line.

4. Type your e-mail message into the text box below the Subject line. If you want to add interest to your text, you can change the typeface, its size, make it Bold, Italic, Underlined, or change colors by using the format bar at the top of the text box. Want to get fancy? Try these tricks on for size:

1. *Highlight the text by clicking your mouse button (and holding it down) at the beginning of the text you want to edit.*

2. *Keep the mouse button down as you drag the mouse pointer across the text.* Lift your finger off the mouse button when you come to the end of the text you want to fancy up.

3. *As shown in **Figure** 3-9, select the attribute you want to apply from the format bar.* In this example, I plan to change the typeface (or font).

4. *Select the font (or color if you're using the color selector) by clicking it, and magically your text will change.*

Click a tool to change the look of your text.

Figure 3-9

5. When you finish writing and formatting your e-mail, click the Send button in the upper-left corner of the e-mail form.

Speaking the Social Networking Language

Chapter 4

You probably suspect that the online social network includes a whole lot more than Twitter and Facebook. And you're right! I suspect that once you get involved on the Web, you're going to want to spread your wings and take off to some other fun venues.

There are quite a few more sites (other than Facebook and Twitter) where you might want to participate with your friends. In this chapter, I give you a very quick overview of the most fun sites I've found in the *interwebs,* or *worldwide webbytubes* — both terms are slang for the Internet. Just to keep you up on what the cool kids say and where they hang.

So, in no special order . . . .

Get ready to . . .

➡ Gather on Facebook 64

➡ Communicate through Twitter 66

➡ Find a Spot on MySpace 68

➡ Get Connected on LinkedIn... 69

➡ See It All on YouTube 70

➡ Have Your Say on BlogSpot 71

➡ Share Photos on Flickr 73

➡ Stream Music on Pandora 73

➡ Watch TV and Movies on Hulu............................... 75

Gather on Facebook

Since a large section of this book is about Facebook, I won't go into a lot of detail, but know that as of October 2012 the site gets one billion (with a 'B') visitors per month. That's a lot of people. You never know who is going to show up on the pages.

Facebook is a place where you can find your family (I just connected with distant relatives across the country), new people with common hobbies and ideas, as well as old school chums. Best of all? You can view old friends' photos and see how they aged over the years. Since anyone over the age of 13 with a valid e-mail address can join, most kids are members. Which gives us parents a nice benefit: We can benevolently "stalk" our kids' and grandkids' pages to see some of what they're doing and watch out for them a bit. (I love looking at my daughter's page.)

Facebook is a community where you can share online contact on a daily basis. You can check in at any time and see what's happening in your friends' and family's world. The benefit of Facebook over Twitter is that you can see all your friends' posts on one page — your home page.

Figure 4-1 shows my profile page. I've been a Facebook member for quite a while so there's always lots happening on my page.

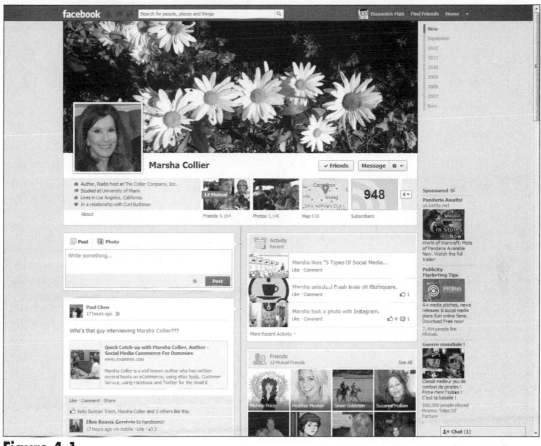

Figure 4-1

Figure 4-2 shows you the Fan Page that the *For Dummies* people set up for me. You can find Fan Pages for some of my favorite public figures, products, and businesses. Joining a Fan Page makes you part of an online community; the posts that the pageholder makes will appear on your home page, just like the posts from your friends. Feel free to find my pages on Facebook and post, I always love meeting my readers.

Figure 4-2

Communicate through Twitter

Have you sent a text message on your phone? If not, it's time to get with it; people send more text messages than they make phone calls these days. As far back as September 2008, Nielsen reported that a typical U.S. mobile subscriber placed or received 204 phone calls each month. In comparison, the average mobile customer sent or received 357 text messages per month (a 450% increase over the number of text messages during the same period in 2006).

Twitter is basically an SMS (for Short Message Service) on the Internet. I'll tell you more about it in Part III of this book, but I know you'll have lots of fun checking in every day to see what the rest of the world has to say.

Figure 4-3 shows my Twitter profile page, along with some of my *tweets* — the online term for Twitter posts or short messages. Though these can't go over 140 characters, you may be surprised at how much information fits into that format. It makes you a more concise writer.

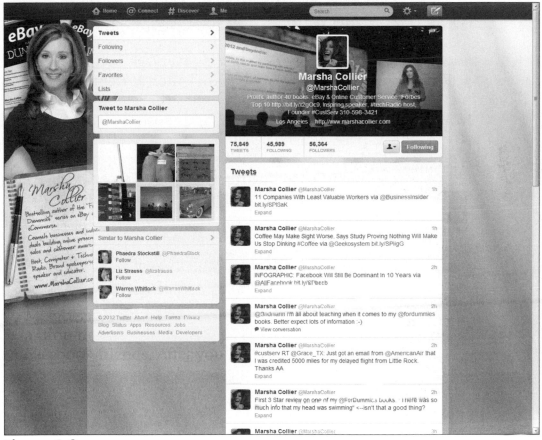

Figure 4-3

After you set up a Twitter account, you can start to "follow" other Twitter members (a process I explain in Chapter 12) and have other members follow you, as well. Once you begin to tweet, you will be able to have real-time conversations with people from the online community that you build this way.

Find a Spot on MySpace

MySpace was the first online social-media community to gain wide usage. It was the most popular social networking site in 2006 but was overtaken by Facebook two years later. It's rumored that MySpace has approximately 30 million (at one time 300 million) unique active users in the United States who are heavily engaged on the site.

MySpace has had a tough time finding its place in the world in the wake of the success of Facebook and Twitter. It went quickly from media darling and flashpoint for online criticism to an also-ran. Nowadays you'll mostly find bands and musicians promoting their works on MySpace, which is great if you're interested in discovering new music. Otherwise most of the action is taking place on other sites. I have a page on MySpace (**Figure 4-4**) that I visit every once in a while, but very few of my friends are active on the site.

Figure 4-4

So if time is somewhat of the essence (who really has spare time any-way?), MySpace might not be on your list of sites to visit. It's really not my cup of tea anymore.

Get Connected on LinkedIn

If you have (or had) a business career, I know you're going to love LinkedIn. It's a business-oriented social network with over 60 million users. If you have a job, you should be on the site. If you're currently "at liberty," semi-retired, or interested in consulting, you should also be on the site. Just think — you can probably connect with most of the colleagues and heavy hitters you've worked with over the years. Your friends may be connected to some smart new folks who just might be looking for your kind of experienced help.

After you register with LinkedIn, you can upload your resume, fill in information about yourself and your talents, and look for former acquaintances whom you've lost track of. You can search (try to remember everyone you've ever worked with) and connect with people you know and trust in business. These become your *connections*. You can invite anyone (whether a site user or not) to become a connection.

 Connections are not automatic. When you locate someone you know on LinkedIn, you have to ask them to connect with you. And don't attempt to connect with someone you don't know. Instead, find someone you already know, connect with him or her, and let that person connect you with new parties. That's the purpose of making connections.

My LinkedIn profile is shown in **Figure** 4-5. I enjoy being connected to the people I've worked with and get notices when they change jobs, update their profiles, or join one of the many groups on the site.

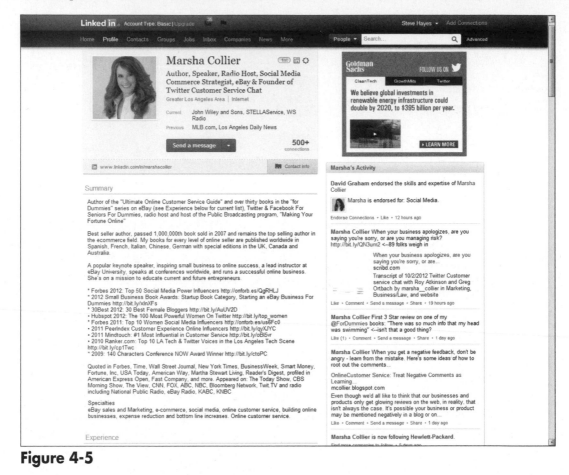

Figure 4-5

See It All on YouTube

You're going to love YouTube — a video-sharing Web site where users can upload and share videos. You can browse almost any subject and find a video you'll enjoy. Want to watch a Harrier take off from an aircraft carrier? Check. Want to see Susan Boyle's performance from *Britain's Got Talent*? Check.

Want to see your grandchild take his first steps? That's up to your son or daughter. Most content on YouTube is uploaded by individuals, but the major media corporations including CBS, BBC, and other organizations offer some of their videos on the site. YouTube is the fourth most visited Web site on the Internet, right behind Google, Yahoo! and Facebook.

I really hope you set up an account on YouTube. You don't have to register to watch videos, but if you'd like to comment and rate videos, you need to have an account. *Entertainment Weekly* magazine put YouTube on its "Best of the Decade" list, saying, "Providing a safe home for piano-playing cats, celeb goof-ups, and overzealous lip-synchers since 2005." It's really a lot of fun!

When you register on the site, you get your own Channel. **Figure 4-6** shows my channel and some of my favorite videos. I just know you'll spend hours on the site watching vintage commercials, TV shows, and more.

Figure 4-6

Have Your Say on BlogSpot

Have you ever considered writing a blog? The term *blog* is a shortened version of *Web-log*, originally a place where people would write and post short stories on the Web. Your blog could be that (short stories) — or a personal journal, random musings, or writings devoted to a specific subject (perhaps a hobby of yours)? It's free to set up and run a blog on Blogspot.com.

As you join more social networking sites, you can link to any blogs as you post them. And you may be surprised at the number of readers you draw. You could develop your own community where regular readers comment on your blog posts (if you wish).

I have a blog on Blogspot (see **Figure** 4-7). Check it out — maybe you'll get an idea of what you'd like to write on yours.

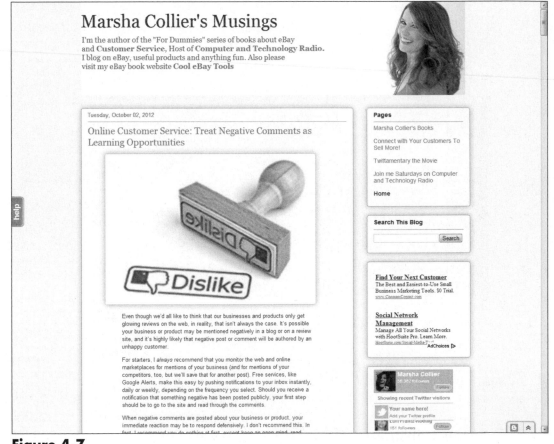

Figure 4-7

Share Photos on Flickr

Flickr is a photo- and video-sharing site that's been on the Web since 2004. In 2005, the site was acquired by Yahoo! — and now you can join Flickr for free and upload photos to share with your friends and family. If you already have a Yahoo! e-mail address, that will become your user name on Flickr. Once you set up your account on Flickr, you can change your screen name to a nickname or your own name.

When you post photos on Flickr, you can *tag* them so your friends and family can find the photos by doing a search for your name or keyword. Tagging is a way to use keywords or names to identify important points about your uploaded images — for example, who's in a photo, where it was taken, and so on. **Figure** 4-8 shows some photos taken on my trip to France. You can use your screen name to find your photo stream (assuming your screen name is your given name) or photos where other people have tagged you by name in their images.

 If you join as a Pro member (for $24.95 a year), you won't have to look at ads, and you can upload an unlimited number of images.

Stream Music on Pandora

Visiting Pandora.com is like having a radio in your computer. When you arrive at the home page, just type in a favorite song or artist, and Pandora will build a radio station for you; it will broadcast songs that you will like. (I promise).

This magic result is based on the Music Genome Project, the most comprehensive analysis of music ever undertaken. Pandora's team of 50 musician-analysts listens to music, one song at a time, to study and collect hundreds of details on every song. According to the Pandora site, it takes the analysts "20-30 minutes per song to capture all of the little details that give each recording its magical sound — melody, harmony, instrumentation, rhythm, vocals, lyrics, and more — close to 400 attributes!"

Figure 4-8

Amazing, no? Once you register, you can create up to 100 stations to fit your many moods. If the music Pandora selects isn't just what you want, let the team know with a click of your mouse and they'll refine the choices selected for your station.

Figure 4-9 shows that I started a Lady Gaga channel, and it's coming up with just the sort of music I want to listen to right now.

PANDORA®
internet radio

register | sign in

Help

Register for FREE to save your stations and access Pandora anytime, anywhere.

register now

Create a New Station...

Your Stations

Poker Face Radio

add variety.. | options ▼

Starstruck

by: Lady Gaga
on: The Fame

Close

buy

To start things off, we'll play another song by Lady Gaga that is musically similar to "Poker Face", featuring electronica influences, a subtle use of paired vocal harmony, repetitive melodic phrasing, extensive vamping and minor key tonality.

Why we're not playing "Poker Face"

About This Music

Your Profile

Genre Stations

Mobile & Home

Video Series

Here's more great stuff to help you enjoy the sounds you love and explore the wider world of music.

Try one.

Your Concert Listings
Find Shows Now

Station Gifting
Make a station for a friend

On Your Mobile Phone
Find Your Phone

Music Festival Guide
Explore Now

Figure 4-9

Watch TV and Movies on Hulu

Having a quiet night? Point your Web browser over to www.hulu.com, where you can find TV shows and movies online — from old favorites to the latest. It's a great place to catch up on shows that you may have missed from your favorite series. You'll find commercial-supported streaming video of TV shows and movies from NBC, Fox, ABC, and many other networks and studios.

When you arrive on the Hulu site, you see promotions for the latest shows added to the site, as shown in **Figure 4-10**. You can browse, by title, the thousands of TV shows and movies on the site by using the buttons at the top of the page.

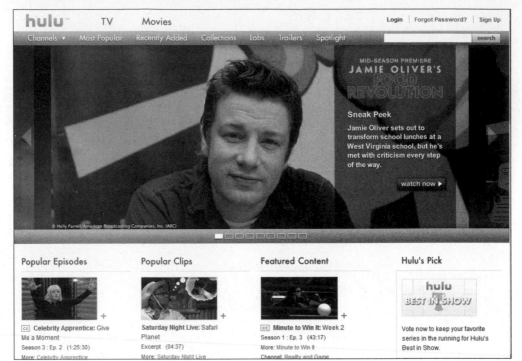

Figure 4-10

Trust me, you're going to love this site. So excuse me for a moment, I'm going to watch one of the 72 episodes of the old *Mary Tyler Moore* show.

Part II
Putting Your Face onto Facebook

The 5th Wave   By Rich Tennant

"I know it's a short profile, but I thought
'King of the Jungle' sort of said it all."

Preparing Your Facebook Profile

Chapter 5

You've heard about it. Your kids and maybe (if you have them) grandkids all have Facebook pages, and now it's your turn. I think that Facebook is the best first place to start connecting online because of the friendly atmosphere. I bet you'll be surprised when you see how many of your friends, past co-workers, and perhaps even past romantic interests await your contact.

To get yourself into the action, you need to sign up and put together your Facebook *profile*, which is where everyone looks to learn more about you. You don't have to fill in your profile information all at once, so don't worry that it's going to be a time consuming task. After you sign up, your Profile page awaits your visits for leisurely updates.

Getting started on Facebook may seem daunting. But when you're ready to take the plunge, I can help you to discover what needs to be done. This chapter lays out all the Facebook setup instructions in sets of easy steps that enable you to master the basics before jumping in with both feet.

By the time you're done reading these pages, you'll have all the knowledge and tools necessary to navigate the site like a pro. All you need

Get ready to . . .

➡ Sign Up for a Facebook Account 80

➡ Find Friends Initially 82

➡ Add Your Personal Information 84

➡ Upload Your Profile Photo 85

➡ Confirming You Are You 90

➡ Fill Out Other Profile Information 91

➡ Go Back to Edit Your Profile Later 96

to add are friends and family! I tell you more about making a Facebook connection with friends and family in Chapter 7.

Let's get moving.

Sign Up for a Facebook Account

1. Open your Internet browser and type in the URL (Universal Resource Locator, the Web address) for Facebook, **www.facebook.com**. When you arrive on the Facebook home page, you find the Sign Up area, as shown in **Figure 5-1**, which asks you to fill in several important facts:

- **Your first and last name.** D'oh, that's the very easiest part.

- **Your e-mail address.** You may have more than one e-mail address, but decide which one will become the hub for your Facebook doings, and enter that address where prompted.

- **Your password.** A very important feature, your password is private, and *encrypted* (a technical way of hiding what you type from anyone other than the inner workings of the site itself — think Jack Bauer from the TV show 24). Never give your password to anyone. You might want to make note of it for your own reference; write it down and put it in a safe place (*not* taped to your computer monitor). You'll have to know your password to sign in to your Facebook account.

- **Your gender.** Okay, this is probably the easy part. Nothing much to decide on here.

- **Your birth date, including the year.** Click the down arrow next to the drop-down menus and select your month, date, and year of birth. Facebook requests your actual date of birth to encourage authenticity and provide only age-appropriate access to content.

 If you're a bit shy of exposing your *real* age, don't feel alone. My age is a secret that I guard tighter than the feds guard the gold at Fort Knox. There is a way around the Facebook requirement. If you use the drop-down menu to select your birth month and date, you can just indicate a year waaaaay back in history. In **Figure 5-1**, I selected a pretty outrageous year — 1905. (Heh, that'll keep 'em guessing.)

facebook

Email or Phone

Password

Log In

Keep me logged in   Forgot your password?

Sign Up
It's free and always will be.

First Name:	Susan
Last Name:	Collier
Your Email:	boss@collierad.com
Re-enter Email:	boss@collierad.com
New Password:	••••••
I am:	Female
Birthday:	Dec 4 1905

Why do I need to provide my birthday?

By clicking Sign Up, you agree to our Terms and that you have read our Data Use Policy, including our Cookie Use.

Sign Up

Create a Page for a celebrity, band or business.

Things that connect us

We honor the everyday things that bring us together and celebrate people everywhere opening up and connecting. Share ›

English (US) Español Português (Brasil) Français (France) Deutsch Italano العربية हिन्दी 中文(简体) 日本語 …

Facebook © 2012 · English (US)

Mobile · Find Friends · Badges · People · Pages · About · Create an Ad · Create a Page · Developers · Careers · Privacy · Cookies · Terms · Help

Fill in your facts and click here.

Figure 5-1

2. After you enter the information in Step 1, click the Sign Up button.

3. Facebook then lands you on a page designed to lead you through a step-by-step process of adding friends, finding even more friends, and filling in profile information (including your picture).

 I cover Facebook's prescribed friend-finding process in the upcoming sections, but I want you to know that you also have the option to skip some of the steps and come back to them later.

Find Friends Initially

1. Facebook takes you to a Find Your Friends page — not unlike the one shown in **Figure 5-2**.

Step 1 Find your friends	Step 2 Profile Information	Step 3 Profile Picture

Are your friends already on Facebook?
Many of your friends may already be here. Searching your email account is the fastest way to find your friends on Facebook. See how it works.

✉ Windows Live Hotmail		Find Friends
Y! Yahoo!		Find Friends
AOl AOL		Find Friends
✉ Other Email Service		

Your Email:
Email Password:

Find Friends

🔒 Facebook won't store your password.

Skip this step

Click this link to continue setting up your page.

Figure 5-2

2. Facebook prompts you to type in your e-mail address
and your e-mail account password. If you do this, it links
your e-mail account and contacts to Facebook, and
allows you to send Facebook friend invitations en masse.
You could do so, but I suggest you skip this step (by
clicking Skip This Step in the right corner of the screen)
for a few reasons:

- **Privacy.** I'm a big believer in privacy. I don't want to
expose my contacts to the Facebook linking.

- **Find them later.** After you've set up everything, it's
very easy to find people on Facebook, and I'm a fan of
baby steps.

- **Completed Profile.** The invitations go out the
moment you click to invite. It will look so much better after you've added your photo and other profile
information.

I recommend that you click Skip for now, because I
also recommend setting up your Facebook page com-
pletely first — and then finding people you know
and wish to add as friends on Facebook. That way,
when they accept your friend invitation, they can see
your already completed, nicely-laid-out new Profile
page. Having your profile completed shows that you
know what you're doing and are ready to roll! Image
is (almost) everything online.

3. Okay, you may think you have skipped finding friends,
but Facebook won't give up. A pop-up window appears
saying: "People who complete this step usually find up to
20 friends, and Facebook is a lot more fun with friends.
Are you sure you want to skip this step?" Yes please.
Click Skip and move along with the sign-up process.

Add Your Personal Information

1. This is where Facebook content gets *really* personal. Facebook asks you to enter your basic profile information, beginning with

   - **The high school you attended** and your year of graduation. When you begin to type your school name, Facebook suggests schools that match, as shown in **Figure 5-3**.

   - **Your college** (if any) and graduation year.

   - **The employer** you work (or worked) for.

    If you want to keep your age private, you wouldn't choose your year of birth from a drop-down menu when prompted. (I didn't, and Facebook let me proceed.) Of course, if you specify your graduation year(s), that's a pretty big hint about your age. But you knew that.

2. After you enter the requested personal information, a window may pop up with suggested friends. You may want to add some or all of these suggested friends based on your school and employment life. You can choose to befriend any or all by clicking their names. Doing so will *immediately* send a friend request to them. (Be sure you want to connect *before* you click — there's no turning back.)

    If you want, you can skip this step and go on to the next task. You can always search for friends later.

![Facebook profile setup screen showing Step 2 Profile Information with a High School dropdown list of Miami-area schools]

facebook   Susan Collier ▾

Step 1   **Step 2**   **Step 3**
Find your friends Profile Information Profile Picture

Fill out your profile info
This information will help you find your friends on Facebook.

High School: Miam   Class End Year: ▾

College/University: **Miami Beach High School**
                       Miami Beach, Florida · School

Employer: **University of Miami**
                       Coral Gables, Florida · Education

◂ Back   **Southwest Miami Senior High**   Skip **Save & Continue**
                       Miami, Florida · School

                       Miami Northwestern Senior High
                       Miami, Florida · School

                       Miami Norland Senior High
                       Miami, Florida · School

                       North Miami Senior High
                       North Miami, Florida · School

                       North Miami Beach Senior High
Facebook © 2012 · English (US)   North Miami Beach, Florida · School   an Ad · Create a Page · Developers · Careers · Privacy · Cookies · Terms · Help

                       Miami Killian High School
                       Miami, Florida · School

                       Miami Southridge Senior High Sc...
                       Miami, Florida · School

                       Miami Carol City High School
                       School

                                Miam

Choose your school from this list.

Figure 5-3

Upload Your Profile Photo

1. Do you have a picture of yourself on your computer that you'd like to share? If so, follow the simple steps that start here. (If you don't have a photo available and your computer has a camera, skip down to Step 8 for those instructions.)

 Step 3 of the Facebook sign-up process says it's time to either *Upload a Photo* or *Take a Photo* to personalize your profile and home pages. Many people are camera-shy and don't put up a photo for their Facebook friends to see. If that's your inclination, I want to tell you that I think that not posting your picture will make your profile page pretty boring. So why not be a little daring and put up your picture?

2. Click the Upload a Photo link, and the Upload Your Profile Picture dialog box appears and prompts you to select an image file on your computer, as shown in **Figure** 5-4.

Click here to look for a profile picture.

Figure 5-4

3. Click the Browse button to start your picture selection. The File Upload window opens and a directory of your computer's contents will appear. Go to the folder where you store your photos. **Figure** 5-5 shows the folder where I store my pictures.

4. Select an image that you'd like to display on your Facebook profile by clicking it. Be sure your selected photo is no bigger than 4 MB (megabytes) in size. (If you don't know what that means, or can't tell how big your photo is, don't worry; Facebook will reject the photo if it's too large.) The name of the photo you chose should appear at the bottom of the window in the File Name text box.

If you question whether a photo is too large, its file size (in *kilobytes*, or KB) should be next to the filename in your folder. If it's too big, you can preview the photo in a photo editing program (for example, Windows Live Photo Gallery) and crop it to a smaller size.

Note: In this chapter, I am showing you figures of the screens I see on a PC that runs Windows. Depending on what operating system you use on your computer, your screens may look a little different. But don't fear — the steps are the same.

Figure 5-5

5. Click Open, and the picture you chose will begin to make its merry way through the Web to Facebook automatically. (Nice, huh?) As shown in **Figure 5-6**, my photo has uploaded to Facebook.

6. If you don't like the photo you selected, you can always change it later in the Edit My Profile area. (You can find the link to this area under your picture on your Profile page.) To go with a different photograph, simply move your mouse over the top of the photo until you see the words *Remove Your Picture*.

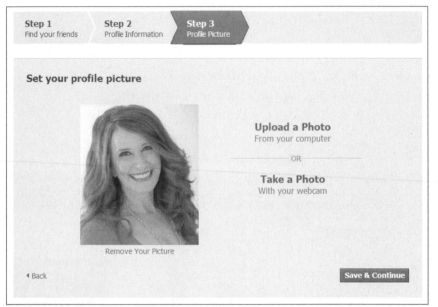

Figure 5-6

7. If you don't already have any photos you like, you can take a picture from your computer Web camera (if you have one). Click Take a Photo with Your Webcam on the Set Your Profile Picture window (refer to **Figure** 5-6).

8. A window appears, as shown in **Figure** 5-7, asking your permission for Facebook to access your camera and microphone. Click the option button next to Allow.

9. Assuming that your webcam is pointing in the right direction, you will now see your image (as you sit at your computer) in the Take a Profile Picture window. Well, you kind of see it. If you want your computer to

remember that you grant access to your camera at any time to Facebook, you must click the check box next to Remember. If you don't want to grant blanket access, that's okay, too — I don't (refer to **Figure** 5-7). So click Close, and there you are, in all your glory.

10. You may now pose for your picture. When you're satisfied with how your picture appears, click the small camera icon at the bottom of your image.

11. Facebook has now taken your picture! If you're happy with it (or as happy as you can be at the moment), click the Save Picture button and your photo will upload to your Facebook profile. (Remember, you can always swap out this picture later.)

Click this option to take your picture.

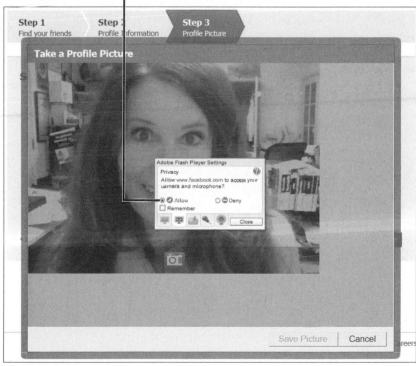

Figure 5-7

Confirming You Are You

1. After the three steps in the Facebook profile-building process are completed (or skipped, based on your choices), you come to a page welcoming you to Facebook, and in a ribbon at the top of the screen you see a notification suggesting you go to your e-mail to complete the sign-up process.

2. Go to your e-mail now and find the e-mail from Facebook. This is their way of being sure that you've supplied the correct e-mail address and you are indeed a living person.

3. Open the e-mail, and it should look similar to the one in **Figure** 5-8. Note that the e-mail has several clickable links that help you further fill out your Facebook profile. Because we have already completed (or skipped) some steps, click the link that says Edit Your Profile. This enables you to add things like personal interests, contact information, and affiliations to your profile.

> **facebook**
>
> Hi Susan,
>
> Your account has been created — now it will be easier than ever to share and connect with your friends.
>
> Sign in to Facebook and start connecting
>
> **Get Started**
>
> **Here are three ways for you to get the most out of it:**
>
> **Find Friends**
> Find people you know on Facebook using our simple tools.
>
> **Upload a Profile Photo**
> Personalize your profile and help your friends recognize you.
>
> **Edit Your Profile**
> Describe personal interests, contact information, and affiliations.
>
> If you have any questions, reference our New User Guide.
>
> Thanks,
> The Facebook Team
>
> Didn't sign up for Facebook? **Please let us know.** Didn't sign up for Facebook? Please let us know:
> http://www.facebook.com/confirmemail.php?e=onlinecustserv%40gmail.com&c=28461&report=1 This message
> was sent to onlinecustserv@gmail.com. Facebook, Inc. Attention: Department 415 P.O Box 10005 Palo Alto CA
> 94303

Click this link.

Figure 5-8

Fill Out Other Profile Information

Clicking the e-mail link brings you to the skeletal stage of the About page of your profile, shown in **Figure 5-9**. Each tiny pen icon links to the tasks that you need to complete to finish posting your profile.

Figure 5-9

At this point, you have a chance to put together the descriptive part of your personal profile. You decide what and how much you share: Make your profile as revealing as you like, or (for a little privacy) as vague. You can get all the privacy you want as you fill out the profile details. Each piece of data can be assigned its own privacy level. By clicking the icon that appears to the right of a text field (see **Figure 5-10**), you see a drop-down menu where you can customize the level of privacy for each bit of information.

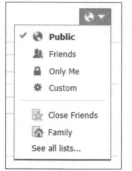

Figure 5-10

1. You've already entered your gender and birth date, so that will be filled in to the Basic Info section (if you added your school and employment info, that area will be prepopulated as well). You now have the opportunity to add more information, such as your relationship status, political and religious views.

 Remember that everything in the Basic Info area is optional.

2. Whatever you choose to share, filling in the blanks is simple. Here are the items to consider:

- **Birthday.** Having the month and day listed is very important. Facebook notifies your Facebook friends about your birthday. They will come to your page and overwhelm you with birthday wishes. So you need to have something here.

  You do have options should you not want to show your birth year (whether real or bogus). You can show your whole birth date, your birth date without the year, or no birthday at all. Check out **Figure 5-11** to see your choices.

Choose how your birthday will appear.

Figure 5-11

- **Relationship Status.** You can leave the relationship space blank, or you have an opportunity to be far more specific (or not) than you might ever have imagined. Besides the boring old *Single* and *Married*, the choices on the drop-down menu also include *In a Relationship, Engaged, In An Open Relationship, Widowed, In a Domestic Partnership* and even *It's Complicated* (which things often are, but note that this term is rather ambiguous and some people may misconstrue it).

  If you indicate that you're in a relationship of some sort, you can then decide whether to list your anniversary date — either for others or simply to remind yourself.

- **Interested In.** You can list whether you're interested in Men or Women and just what you're Looking For from Facebook: Friendship, Dating, A Relationship, Networking — or leave all these boxes unchecked.

- **Languages.** If you speak more than one language, why not let your friends know? Just fill in the name.

- **Political and Religious Views.** In the Political Views text block, you can type in the name of a political party, or a comment that seems funny. In Religion, type in the name of your faith if you wish.

3. After you input all the Basic Info you want to enter, click the Save button.

 The idea isn't to reveal so much about yourself that you eliminate any mystery. It's simply to give others on Facebook a semi-definitive and representative picture of yourself, enough so your personality comes to the surface. You can also delay filling in this information until later if you prefer. You may decide to get the lay of the Facebook land a bit more prior to adding more personal information. Or you might decide never to reveal this stuff at all. It's really entirely up to you.

4. If you have any family members on Facebook whom you want to link to, click Edit in the Relationships and Family box. Type in their name and select the appropriate relationship for that person by clicking the Choose Relationship link. After they confirm to Facebook that you really are related, you get a link to their profile page on yours. Pretty cool.

5. Next, if you haven't already supplied the information, click the Work and Education section link. This section affords you the chance to elaborate on your high-school and college info, as well as what you do (or did) for a living.

The benefit of including this information is that many people search for Facebook friends by schools or workplaces, and an old school chum may find you by performing such a search.

6. To tell your story, edit the About You and the Favorite Quotations boxes. Write up a short bio; people want to know a little about you. Also, keep in mind that people's favorite quotations say a lot about them. Type in a few quotes that you love with the appropriate attributions.

7. Click the Contact Info section link, and the form appears on-screen. You may notice you have a new e-mail address assigned to you by Facebook. People can connect to you through the site by using that address if they so wish, and the e-mail shows up in your messages area (Chapter 7 gives you more information on messages). Your personal e-mail address is already filled in because you input this information at the beginning of the sign-up process.

At this point, you can type in any contact information you want your Facebook friends to see, including your

- **IM (instant message) screen name.** Also, you can choose the IM service you use from the associated drop-down list.

- **Mobile phone and land line numbers.**

- **Address and ZIP code.**

 This is where sharing gets sticky for me. I may make friends on Facebook that I don't want to have my home address and phone number. For the sake of my security, I leave that blank. If I want someone to have that information, they can always send me an e-mail to request it.

- **Website URL.** If you have a blog or a Twitter page, type the URL in here.

Go Back to Edit Your Profile Later

1. When you have your information in place, you may decide to make additions and changes. You can always return to edit your profile information by clicking the About link below your profile photo on your Timeline page.

    Remember that any information you enter about yourself — along with your name and friends list — can be as private or public as you wish.

2. Information that you may consider sensitive is available only to those whom you have befriended, based on your settings. And that's where the privacy and security settings come in. At any time, you can adjust your global or individual privacy settings for contact and profile information by clicking the down arrow in the top right of any Facebook page and then choosing Privacy Settings from the resulting menu. See Chapter 6 for a more complete look at choosing your privacy settings.

Preparing to Share Info

On Facebook, there are three basic levels of privacy: *Friends*, *Friends of Friends*, and *Everyone*. You consistently hold the key to how much, or how little, information about yourself you allow to be accessed on the site. The personal information you choose to share is apart from the publicly available information — such as your name, profile picture, current city, gender, networks, friend list, and pages — that helps friends find and connect with you.

On Facebook, your privacy and security settings work as locks that control access to what's revealed about you, and to whom. In this chapter, I show you how to access and edit your privacy and security settings at any time. The idea behind these settings is to give you full control of your Facebook experience.

Use these settings so you don't have to worry about your personal information falling into the wrong hands — or having prying eyes access something about you that (for whatever reason) you don't want just anybody to know. You are in charge — and can filter who views your information to increase your feelings of security and privacy online.

Chapter

6

Get ready to . . .

➠ Get Your Privacy and Security Settings in Place 98

➠ Meet Your Facebook Home Page 102

➠ Review Your Timeline Page 104

➠ Update Your Status 109

➠ Delete a Status Update or Other Post 110

➠ Add a Photo to Your Timeline 111

➠ Adding Timeline Life Events 112

➠ Share a YouTube Video on Facebook 113

The privacy of your status updates, photos and information can be set as you post them, using the privacy selector on the fly.

Then, with your information secure, you can move on to the fun stuff! This chapter also shows you how to make the most of your Facebook pages, by posting updates and photos, and getting into the conversation. Let's get the tough stuff out of the way first.

Get Your Privacy and Security Settings in Place

1. To start the process of checking your privacy and security settings, look at the top right of the screen on your Facebook page and locate the word *Home*. When you click the down arrow next to Home, a drop-down menu appears, as shown in **Figure 6-1**.

Figure 6-1

 Because Facebook (like any Web site) develops and morphs with new features every day, I recommend that you check out the Facebook blog, `http://blog.facebook.com` often. Facebook staffers (and the founder Mark Zuckerberg) post updates and information on an almost daily basis.

2. Click Privacy Settings in the drop-down menu to go to the Privacy Settings page, which gives you a few options. The privacy settings enable you to control who can see your profile information, contact information, application and Web-site data, and searches. Also, you can control who can interact with you on Facebook through the Block List. You click each section name to get to the settings for that section. **Figure 6-2** shows you the individually selectable settings on the page. Notice that when you click to edit each section, you will see the selections you made while signing up or Facebook's recommended settings.

How You Connect Control how you connect with people you know.		Edit Settings
Timeline and Tagging Control what happens when friends tag you or your content, or post on your timeline.		Edit Settings
Ads, Apps and Websites Manage your settings for ads, apps, games and websites.		Edit Settings
Limit the Audience for Past Posts Limit the audience for posts you shared with friends of friends or Public		Manage Past Post Visibility
Blocked People and Apps Manage the people and apps you've blocked.		Manage Blocking

Figure 6-2

3. Click the Edit Settings link to make any changes. When you arrive at the Privacy Settings page there will be a link to edit your basic info. Clicking that link will allow you to make alterations to your profile and contact information settings.

4. A graphic on the page shows your default privacy settings when using the rare mobile app that does not include an inline audience selector. Fear not, the most popular mobile operating systems: iPhone, Android and Windows phone offer the privacy selector. By clicking on the globe icon, you can choose who will see your post as pictured on my Android phone in **Figure 6-3**. When you choose the Custom option, a separate box pops up where you can make your posts available to only you, friends or to certain people (whom you specify). You can also choose to block certain people from seeing this information.

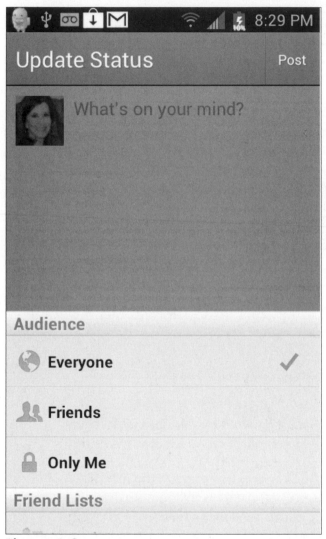

Figure 6-3

When editing the sections on this page, simply click the button at the end of a sub-category and choose a setting from the drop-down list. The standard settings are Everyone, Friends of Friends, Friends, or Customize.

Note: If you have a special situation — for example, if you've joined a Facebook network — you may see other options in this list.

Here's a little more about each section of the Privacy Settings:

- **How You Connect:** Here you control who can send you friend request and messages.

- **Timeline and Tagging:** Part of the fun of Facebook is that other members can post comments, pictures, and video. If another member tags you in a posted item, it will also appear on your wall. Here's the area where you decide who can post (and comment) on your wall and who can view photos of you.

5. Click the Done or Back to Privacy button after you edit any settings to return to the main Privacy Settings page where you find links to the other areas you may want to customize. They are

- **Ads, Apps and Websites:** In this section, you put into place controls on what your friends can share about you when they're using applications and Web sites on Facebook. You can also block certain applications from accessing your information and contacting you; such applications include games, causes, and surveys. If you simply don't want to be bothered, you can choose to ignore application invites from specific friends.

  On this page, you will also be able to edit Public Search. This privacy setting controls who can see your name or profile information as search results on Facebook. This setting also indicates whether to allow search engines such as Google to access your publicly available information. Click the Edit Settings button and then click See Preview, as I did in **Figure 6-4**, to view what your results might look like when someone finds you from a search engine.

**Marsha Collier
is on Facebook.**

To connect with Marsha, sign up for Facebook today.

Sign Up   Log In

Marsha Collier   ·· Add Friend   ·· Subscribe

Favorites

Music

Paul   Stacye   The Common

Wrong Marsha Collier? Try Again

Marsha Collier   Search

Others Named Marsha Collier

Marsha Collier

Figure 6-4

- **Block Lists:** Click the Edit Your Lists link under Block Lists. If there are some folks you'd really rather not interact with on Facebook, this setting allows you to block them from access. Simply type in each name and/or e-mail address you want to block, and then click the Block this User button.

Meet Your Facebook Home Page

1. You have two pages on Facebook: your home page and your Timeline. You can select the one you want to view by clicking either Home or your name in the upper-right corner of any Facebook page. Clicking Home brings you to your personal home page; **Figure 6-5** shows mine. Your home page has links for just about anything you want to do or see on Facebook. In the center of the page is a column for News Feeds, featuring your friends updates.

2. The news feed shows the updates your friends have posted that are getting the most attention with replies by default. You may click the arrow next to the word Sort at the top of your feed to view Most Recent posts if you'd like to see each post from each of your friends, in the order of posting.

Toolbar links are here.   Activities are here.

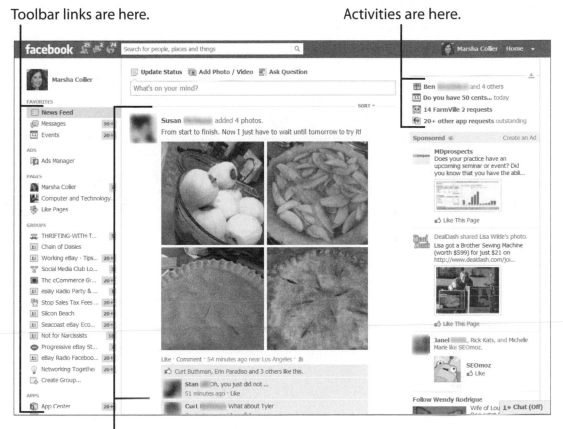

Updates from friends are here.

Figure 6-5

3. You also have other sections with links to information and activities on the right side of this page. Click the links (scroll down the page) to find how many requests are pending in each category — or simply to explore all that's available on Facebook. The home page sections include

- **Birthdays:** Click the birthdays link to see which of your friends has a birthday today. By clicking the link you will see their names and be able to post a happy birthday wish that will post directly to their page.

- **Events:** In the Events heading you can click to see links to upcoming events (in chronological order) that you've been invited to.

- **Requests:** Further down in the right-hand column, you may find game and app requests.

- **Toolbar links:** On the left side (under a thumbnail of your profile picture), you see links to take you to your personal destinations on Facebook, as well as a link to Chat. (If you are offline — not open for chat as described in Chapter 7 — Facebook prompts you to Turn on chat.) These links will vary from person to person depending on your participation in pages, Groups and Apps.

Review Your Timeline Page

1. Click your name at the top-right of any Facebook page, and you arrive on your Timeline page showing your public profile. Your Facebook Timeline is designed to chronicle your travels and activities. It can show how you categorize your life and times and digitally document your entire life, should you wish. The page, as you see it, is exactly the way it looks to your friends when they visit your page. Notice that there are four boxes just below your name. The four boxes are just the start; you can always add more as you become a Facebook denizen.

Figure 6-6 shows you the page of a brand new Facebook member with not much filled in. **Figure 6-7** shows mine, something closer to what your page will look like once you have been on Facebook for a while.

Click this to find a cover photo.

![facebook profile page screenshot showing Susan Collier's timeline with "Add a Cover" button highlighted on the right side]

Figure 6-6

2. In **Figure 6-7**, you see a large photo at the top. This is
your cover image. Your Cover photo is the first thing that
people see when they come to your Facebook page. Your
Profile photo appears in the lower left side, inset into the
cover. You can use a personal photo or one you find on a
website that shares Facebook cover photos — pretty
much any photo that expresses your mood at the time.
Click Add a Cover on the right side of your page.

 After you have stored photos on Facebook (see
Chapter 8) you can change your cover to any of these
other photos as well as upload a new one.

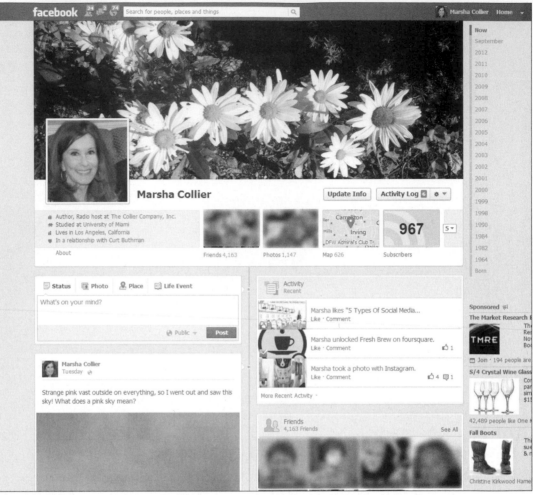

Figure 6-7

3. You will be prompted to Upload a photo, and a window on your computer pops up. Go to the folder that holds your pictures, select one, click Upload, and the photo appears on your page.

 The photo appears as 851 pixels wide by 315 deep — but I wouldn't be too concerned about the exact size; just stick to horizontal format pictures. Facebook will enlarge your photo to fit the space if it's too small. But the photo has to be at least 720 pixels wide, or

Facebook will ask you to select a different one. If your image is larger than 315 pixels in height, you have the option to reposition your image.

4. Over your image, you'll see the words Drag to Reposition Cover. To center your photo vertically *mouse over* (hover your mouse pointer in that area); the cursor turns into a hand icon to drag the image up or down until you feel it's centered just the way you want it.

5. Click the Save Changes button, and your image will appear at the top of your Facebook Timeline page.

6. The four boxes that appear on your page are:

- **Friends:** As you accumulate friends on Facebook, teeny versions of their profile pictures appear here. When you click the box, a page with clickable links and pictures of all your friends will appear.

- **Photos:** Here's where you see photos of you that you've posted, and images of you that other people have posted. Photos magically appear here when a friend tags you in a picture. (Check out Chapter 8 for the how-to information on adding photos and tagging friends.) Click here to go to a page with all your photos and albums.

- **Map:** Every photo or Life Event that you post can be geo-tagged when uploaded from a mobile device. Geo-tagging marks the items with the location in which they occurred. If you post photos and events from your computer, Facebook lets you tag the city, state, or country. This link will lead you to a map, like mine in **Figure 6-8**, pinned from all the places you've posted.

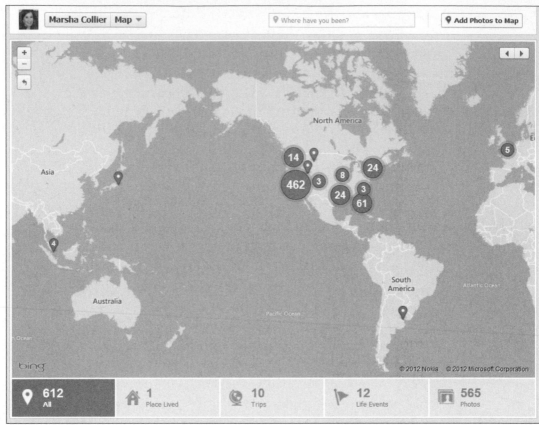

Figure 6-8

- **Likes:** This box lets your Facebook friends know which business, fan, or group pages you've given the "thumbs up" to.

7. You have additional tabs on your Profile page visible by clicking the number followed by a down arrow on the end of your tabs. When you do, a drop-down shows hidden boxes for Subscriptions (If you find some interesting folks you don't know well enough to friend, you can still subscribe to their Timelines), Events (you have been invited to) and Notes.

Update Your Status

1. Here's where the fun really begins. In the thin, long rectangular box that appears at the top of either of your Facebook pages, type in your *status* — some words about what's going on with you at the moment. Inside the status-update box, you see the question *What's on your mind?* To answer the question — called *posting* — click inside the box and type any message you wish.

 Most people use the update feature to let people know what they're doing at that given moment — so often you see quick notes such as "Baking a cake for my in-laws" or "Going to work out on the treadmill."

2. You can attach videos, photos or links to interesting pages on the Web. If you're posting your update from your Profile page, you can add places or Life Events. Click the icon representing the item, should you want to attach something to your comment. To attach a Web site link to a status update:

1. Type your status update into the text box.

2. Navigate in another browser tab to the Web site you want to share and select its URL by highlighting it in your browser's address bar. Then copy it by pressing Ctrl + C on your keyboard.

3. Paste the URL below your comments by clicking and then pressing Ctrl + V on your keyboard. A mini-version of your linked page will appear below the comment (see **Figure 6-9**).

4. After the thumbnail of your link appears in the update box, you can delete the URL. The thumbnail contains the link to the article or page.

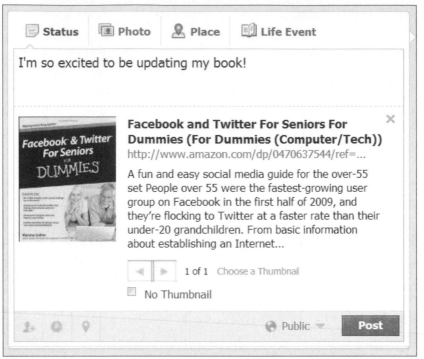

Figure 6-9

3. When you're done typing the message (and attaching a photo, video, or link), check the Privacy selector (click on the small globe icon) to be sure you have chosen who will see the update. Now click the Post button at the bottom right of the status-update section.

 The words you typed in your status update (if you did not attach a link or photo) will appear with your name at the top of your Facebook Timeline stream.

Delete a Status Update or Other Post

1. Removing the current status update from your Profile page is one of the simpler tasks to perform on Facebook. Move your cursor to the upper right-hand corner of the offending status update, and a star and a pencil icon will appear with the words Edit or Remove.

2. Click the pencil, and the option to Delete appears, as shown in **Figure 6-10**. (If someone has shared something to your page, you will have the option to Hide from Timeline).

Click here to delete your post.

Figure 6-10

3. Click Delete and a confirmation window pops up. Confirm you wish to delete the post appears, and it's gone.

Add a Photo to Your Timeline

1. To post a photo to your Timeline, locate the word *Photo* and the row of icons at the top of the status update text box where you see the question *What's on your mind?*

2. Click the Photos icon. Doing this brings up three options: Attach Photo / Video, Use Webcam, and Create Photo Album. The procedure is the same as loading a photo for your Profile page.

3. Click Attach Photo, and you see a box that prompts you to browse for a photo or video on your computer. Click the Choose File button to look for a picture on your computer. After you find a photo, click that photo to select it. Then you can put it up on your Facebook wall by clicking the Post button at the bottom of the status-update box.

Adding Timeline Life Events

1. Life events happen to us all. And in your Timeline status box, you have the opportunity to share your special events with the world (or just with your friends). To add a significant event, click the Life Event link above the status update box.

2. Select one of the five main categories that identifies your event. Facebook will produce a slider menu on the right (as shown in **Figure** 6-11) offering a list of options in the main categories.

Figure 6-11

3. Select the category you wish to add and fill out the form that pops up, including the city and state in which the event occurred.

4. Add a photo. (You can upload a fresh one or select from photos already uploaded.)

5. Specify the Privacy setting by clicking the small down arrow to the left of the Save button.

6. When you're all done, click Save and the event will be part of your Timeline and on your map.

 Clicking a year (or decade) in the Timeline navigation at the right of your Page takes you to that specific point in your Timeline.

Share a YouTube Video on Facebook

1. So you just watched a video on YouTube and you can't wait to show it to all your friends. Well, it turns out that Facebook is the perfect place to show a video to the maximum number of friends in the minimum amount of time. Start out by going to YouTube (www.youtube. com) and clicking the video you want to share. Beneath the screen that's showing the actual video, you should see a Share button. Click it, and you get several buttons you can click to share the video on various social networking sites, including Twitter, MySpace, StumbleUpon, and (you guessed it) Facebook.

2. Click the Facebook button, and you're prompted to add a message in a rectangular text box (similar to the status update space). Type in your message, click the Share button at bottom right, and voila! You've posted a video to your Facebook wall.

You can also copy the URL of your video, and then paste it into a status update, as you would when posting any link. See this chapter's earlier task, "Update Your Status" for the steps.

 If you want to upload a video of your own that you have on your computer, you can post it the same way you upload a photo. Just be sure to click the icon of the teeny movie camera in the Attach area.

Connecting with Friends and Family

Chapter 7

Now that your Facebook Timeline page is all set up and people can see who you are, it would make sense to have some friends online to connect with. Facebook can be a lonely place if you don't make friends, so in this chapter, I help you find lots of friends: old and new.

So put on your thinking cap. Think of the various offline connections you have — aside from the people in your daily life (and your family) — think back to friends from previous jobs, church, schools, and maybe even summer camp. (I'm friends on Facebook with the girl who use to pick on me mercilessly when I was a kid; she's not half bad now!)

Ready? This is going to be fun.

Get ready to ...

➡ Make the Navigation Bar Your First Stop..................... 116

➡ Find a Friend with Facebook Search................. 118

➡ Send a Friend Request 121

➡ Find Friends in Other Friends' Lists........................ 122

➡ Respond to a Friend Request 123

➡ Connect with a Facebook Network 125

➡ Send Private Messages to Friends 127

➡ Retrieve a Private Message... 129

➡ Chat with Your Friends......... 130

➡ Post Updates on a Friend's Wall 132

➡ Comment on a Friend's Status 134

➡ Post a Note........................ 135

➡ Remove Messages from Your Wall............................ 136

Make the Navigation Bar Your First Stop

1. Whenever you visit Facebook, you see a blue bar at the top of the page. This Navigation bar, as shown in **Figure 7-1**, appears on all Facebook pages. The Navigation bar does just what its name implies: It allows you to navigate to different pages on Facebook quickly. From here, you can get a brief view of what's going on with your Facebook account. At the top left are small red squares over icons that may have white numbers in them.

See requests, messages, and notifications here.

Figure 7-1

2. Check out the activities available from the Navigation bar. From **Figure 7-1**, I can see that I have 26 friend requests, 2 new messages and 67 Notifications. Clicking these icons will do different things (keep in mind that anything you can do by clicking these icons you can also do from your home page):

- **Friend Requests:** When you click here, you'll see a drop-down menu showing the people who have requested your friendship online. You may click on their names to go directly to their timelines.

- **Messages:** You have this many messages from other Facebook members in your message area. You may view previews of their messages here, and click to go directly to each message.

- **Notifications:** If someone has posted a note on your wall, commented on a post of yours, commented on a picture you're in, it's a notification. Click here and you'll get a drop-down menu like the one in **Figure 7-2**.

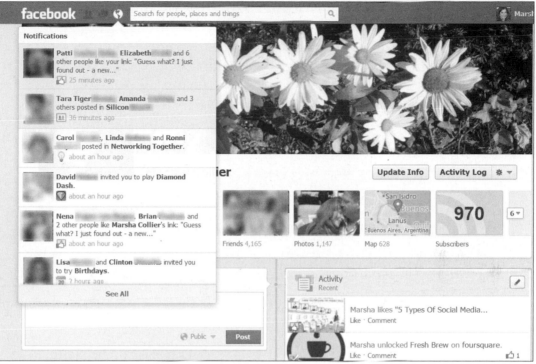

Figure 7-2

3. Are you looking for something on Facebook? A friend, your local coffee shop (if it has a fan page, it may post coupons), your favorite movie or author? Try out the Facebook search feature. Just start typing the name or topic in the Search box, and a drop down list appears. As you type the words, Facebook uses the drop-down list to suggest a name (or topic) that matches what you are typing. If you see what you're looking for, click that name or phrase. If the name doesn't show up, click See More Results at the bottom of the drop-down list and search from there.

 If you don't see a See More Results link at the bottom of the menu, odds are there's no match on Facebook. You can still try to search by clicking the little magnifying glass in the Search box.

4. Clicking the Home link takes you to your Home page, the hub for your news feed and all your invitations and (most important) the organization area on the left side of the screen. This area gives you access to other Facebook activities, including photos and your friends. (Later sections in this chapter cover these activities.)

5. Clicking on your name links you to your Timeline page. From there, you can see what your friends have posted on your wall as well as edit any information on the page.

6. Next is a down-pointing arrow — unless you haven't signed up any friends on Facebook — in that case, you will see the words *Find Friends* before the Home link. (Read the next section, where I help you with finding friends.) Once you've gotten connected to a few friends, what you see here is only a menu to your settings.

Click the down arrow to select which area you wish to set your preferences to control how you operate on Facebook — including how private you want to be. (I cover the details in Chapter 6.)

Find a Friend with Facebook Search

1. Think of a small group of your friends and write down a list. Then sign in to your Facebook account; you'll land on your Home page. From here, you have two ways of finding people; start by using the Search box. Type one of your friend's names in the Search box, as I've done in **Figure** 7-3. Just as when you're searching for anything on Facebook, a drop-down list appears — this one with semi-matching names.

If you're not sure how to spell your friend's name, just type in as many characters of it as you think may be right. Facebook will pick up the slack. Alternatively, you can type in your friend's last known e-mail address, but people change e-mail addresses so often these days, that it might not be valid anymore.

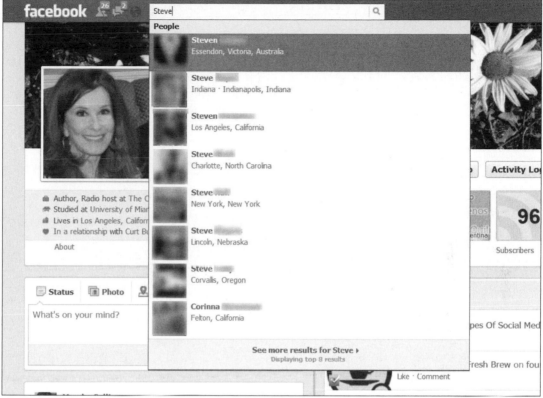

Figure 7-3

2. If your friend is not on the suggested list, click the See More Results link. You'll then see a page (or many pages) with results that match what you've typed in. You should be able to find your friend if he or she is a member of Facebook.

3. Remember that I said there were two ways to find friends? Look at the blue bar at the top of the page for the Friend Requests (two people) icon. Click the icon and a drop-down menu appears, showing any friend requests you may have (also to the right of the words Friend Requests). Click there and you will come to a page with a tool that allows you to Add Personal Contacts as Friends (shown in **Figure 7-4**). Select any of the e-mail services listed and type in your e-mail ID and password. Facebook imports your contacts automatically.

Figure 7-4

This Facebook import contacts feature is called Friend Finder. It's perfectly safe and Facebook does not store your password. But even so, I don't like it; here are some reasons why:

- I'm a stickler for privacy and do not wish to share my online contact lists with anyone.

- Friend Finder makes automatic connections based on the e-mail addresses in your address book. Facebook says: "Facebook won't share the email addresses you import with anyone, but we will store them on your behalf and may use them later to help others search for people or to generate friend suggestions for you and others." If you don't want them to store this information, visit

this page to Remove All Imported Contacts:
`https://www.facebook.com/contact_`
`importer/remove_uploads.php`.

4. If the features of Friend Finder are fine with you, feel free to add your online contact list. I can tell you that Facebook won't lie, but be sure you read every notification message before agreeing to any Facebook activity.

Other links at the left show you which friends have recently made changes to their Timeline pages. The changes they have made are highlighted to the right of their names.

Send a Friend Request

1. When you find someone on Facebook you'd like to add as a friend, doing so is a pretty simple task. After clicking the link to your prospective friend's Timeline page, you may see an Add Friend box next to the name.

2. Click the Add Friend button, and it changes to blue with the words Friend Request Sent as in **Figure 7-5**. Also, a window pops up, suggesting you add this person to one of your groups of friends. In addition, this window gives you the option to cancel the request.

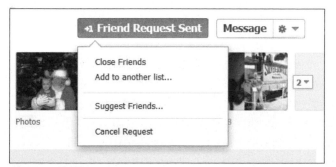

Figure 7-5

3. After you send your request, a friend request is posted to the recipient's Facebook notifications. Your prospective new friend also receives an e-mail notice with an easy link she can click to respond.

Find Friends in Other Friends' Lists

1. Odds are that the friends you have on Facebook are connected to people you may know. Would you like to make those people your friends on Facebook, too? It's easy. Facebook Timeline pages have Friends boxes you can find below the cover photo (unless the member has chosen to block the box from view). If you have Facebook friends in common, you'll see the number of mutual friends on the box, as shown in **Figure 7-6**.

Figure 7-6

2. By clicking the box, you can view all of your friend's connections in a new window (see **Figure 7-7**). And you will see an expandable box with Mutual Friends above all their Facebook friends.

3. You can search through the list (looking for a specific person) in two ways: by typing the person's name in the search box and clicking the magnifying glass, or by scrolling down the list and viewing each friend individually. Another way to search is by clicking the arrow next to the magnifying glass, which drops a menu (shown in **Figure 7-8**) of search qualifiers. When someone is not already your friend on Facebook, to the right of each entry is an Add Friend link that you can click to send a friend request.

Figure 7-7

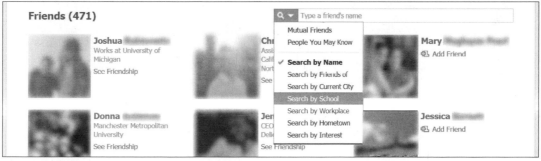

Figure 7-8

Respond to a Friend Request

1. When people know you're a Facebook member, someone is going to want to be your friend on Facebook. There are two ways you will be notified of a friend request: You get a notification via e-mail, or you find out when you log in to your Facebook home page. If you receive your notification via e-mail, just click the link contained in the message and you go directly to the request.

2. When you log in to Facebook, any page offers you a notification area to see your friend requests. The place to check is at the top left of your page, next to the Facebook logo in your toolbar. The button to click resembles the silhouette of two people. If you have a new friend request, you'll see a small red box with a number in it, overlapping the icon. To access your requests, click on icon. **Figure 7-9** shows you my current friend requests.

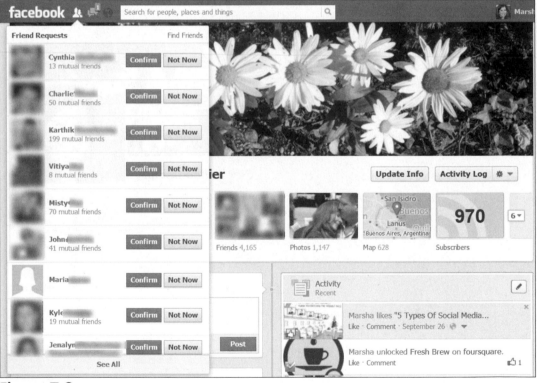

Figure 7-9

3. When you access your friend requests icon, you see your potential friend's photo and name. You also see whether you have any mutual friends with this person (and how many). By clicking the Mutual Friends link under the potential friend's name, you can see the friends you have in common.

4. To respond to a friend request, click one of the two buttons to the right of your potential friend's name. One button reads *Confirm* and one reads *Not Now*. Clicking those buttons allow you to add a friend or to ignore the request quietly.

 When you ignore a friend request, an e-mail isn't sent to the person who placed the request. That person will not know that you chose to ignore him or her, except for the fact that you didn't accept the request. Oops?

Connect with a Facebook Network

1. Facebook gives you the chance to become part of a network. *Networks* (in Facebook-speak) are a group of people who have similar hometowns, backgrounds, or interests. This feature allows you to easily connect with your current or past coworkers or classmates and helps you to be easily identified. To start the simple task of joining a network, click the down facing arrow⇨Account from the top navigation bar.

2. When you arrive at your General Account Settings page, select the Edit link to the left of the word Networks. The Join A Network link appears, as shown in **Figure 7-10**.

facebook   Search for people, places and things   Marsha Collier   Home ▾

General
Security
Notifications
Subscribers
Apps
Mobile
Payments
Facebook Ads
Gifts

You can also visit your privacy
settings or edit your timeline to
control who sees the info there.

General Account Settings

Name	Marsha Collier	Edit
Username	http://www.facebook.com/marsha.collier	Edit
Email	Primary: marsha.collier@gmail.com	Edit
Password	Updated about 9 months ago.	Edit
Networks	Your primary network will appear next to your name.	
	Join a network	

Save Changes   Cancel

| Language | English (US) | Edit |

Download a copy of your Facebook data.

Click this link to enter a city, workplace, school,
or region you'd like to be associated with.

Figure 7-10

3. You have the option to join a network by clicking the
Join A Network link; this will be your main network and
will appear next to your name on your Timeline page.
Enter a city, workplace, school, or region that you would
like to be associated with in the Network Name text box.
The auto-fill feature shows you the names of networks
that match what you're typing. I typed *Los Angeles*
because I live and worked there, and got the results
shown in **Figure 7-11**. My old employer popped up —
and, if I chose to, I could select that entry to become part
of the Los Angeles Daily News network.

 When you select an employer network, you are often
asked for your e-mail address so they can confirm
your employment.

4. After you fill in any required information, click the Join
Network button. Facebook sends your request, and all
you have to do is await confirmation.

Figure 7-11

Send Private Messages to Friends

1. Facebook has a feature that enables you to send private messages to your friends. Think of it like Facebook e-mail, only your personal e-mail address is not revealed. Even better, you can e-mail those whose e-mail addresses you don't know. One way to send a message to a friend is to click the Messages link on the left side of your home page. Facebook takes you to your Messages page, as shown in **Figure 7-12**.

2. Click the New Message button in the top-right corner of this page, and a blank message form opens on your screen, as shown in **Figure 7-13**. Alternatively, you can visit a friend's Facebook Timeline page. Just under the cover photo, you should see a Message box. Click it, and you get the same blank message form.

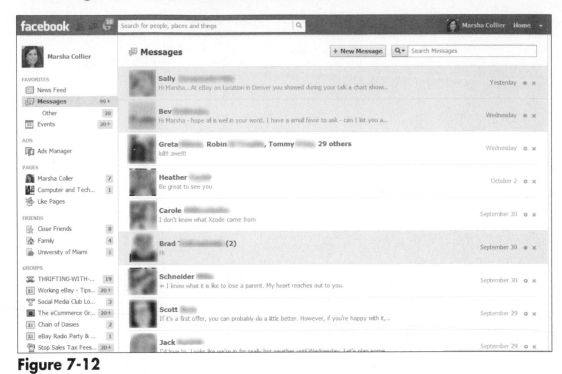

Figure 7-12

Figure 7-13

3. In the blank message form (refer to **Figure 7-13**), address the message by typing your friend's name into the To box. Facebook begins to auto fill names from your friend list as you type. When you find the correct friend, select the name by either clicking it or highlighting it and pressing Enter.

4. For all messages, fill in the Subject and Message text boxes as you would for an e-mail. When you have completed your message, simply click the Send button in the lower-right corner of the New Message form (or click Cancel if you've changed your mind).

 You have options to attach files, photos, videos, and links to your message, as well as a variety of items — depending on whether you subscribe to any Facebook applications.

Retrieve a Private Message

1. More than likely, once you send a message, you'll get a reply. Retrieving and answering private messages is simple. Facebook sends you an e-mail with the message. You can respond by clicking the Respond link on the message.

2. But as with most Facebook tasks, you also have two places on the site where you can retrieve a private message:

- Click the button (that resembles two conversation bubbles) in the toolbar on the top left of your home page, and a drop-down list with a snap shot of your current messages opens (see **Figure 7-14**). Click to select the message you wish to read from the list and you see the full message.

- Click the Messages link on the left side of your home page, and Facebook takes you to your Messages page. It's like your e-mail Inbox. To read a message, simply click it and the full message opens.

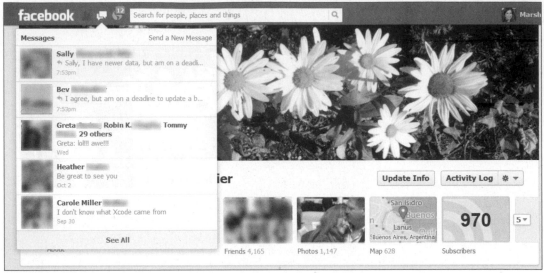

Figure 7-14

Chat with Your Friends

1. You've heard about Instant Messengers (IMs), right? Like AOL Instant Messenger? Well, a *chat session* is Facebook's version of the instant message service. It allows you to chat with friends who are online at the same time you are. To see the friends you have online you can check in two places:

• On the left side of your home page, beneath your messages, you see a Friends Online area.

• At the lower-right corner of any Facebook page, you see a Chat box. Click it, and you see a scrollable list of all your friends who are currently online.

2. If you see someone online that you'd like to speak to and want to start a chat session, click the name of the friend. A chat box opens at the bottom of your screen. After the box opens, type in your message and press Enter. Your message then pops up in the chat box and your session has begun.

3. You can also be on the receiving end of a chat session. If you hear a pop noise, and a small window opens, someone is requesting to chat with you. To respond, type in your message and press Enter. Your message will pop up in the chat box. I'm chatting with a couple of friends in **Figure 7-15**.

Figure 7-15

 If you're just breezing through Facebook and have things to do, you may not want to get involved in a chat session. If this is the case, merely click the Chat link in the lower right of your home page. Then click the cog icon in the right corner and select Turn Off Chat at the bottom of the box that opens. (See **Figure 7-16**.) You will become invisible to all, and you'll be free to go about your Facebook chores undisturbed.

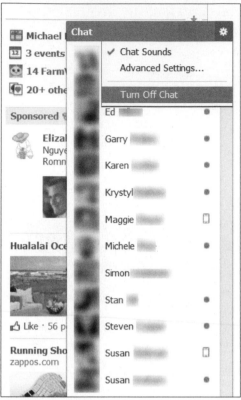

Figure 7-16

Post Updates on a Friend's Wall

1. On your Facebook home page, you'll see notations from your friends' walls. They are put there either with a status update from the person whose wall it is, or by one of their friends posting a message. To post a message on a friend's wall, go to your friend's Facebook Timeline page. Make sure you are on your friend's wall by selecting the Wall tab from the toolbar below their name and above the text box. The text box is filled with a prompt that reads *Write something* in grayed-out letters.

2. To post your message, simply type it in the test box, as I did in **Figure 7-17**. If you'd like to add a picture to your message, click the Photo link and add it. (Find more about attachments in Chapter 8.)

3. When you're done with your message and attachments, click the Post button on the right side under the message box. Voila! Your message is now on display for your friend and potentially all visitors to their page.

If you want to refer to another friend in your posted message, before you type in his or her name, type the @ sign (the symbol for *at*). Then begin to type in the person's name. When the name pops up in the drop-down menu of friends' names that appears (see **Figure 7-18**), click it to create a link to that friend in your post. Your post will then also appear on the linked friend's Timeline page.

Figure 7-17

Figure 7-18

Comment on a Friend's Status

1. If you see a status message your friend has posted and
you'd like to comment on it, it's as simple as 1, 2, 3.
Click the Comment link under the status post. A window
drops down with a blank box in which you can type your
comment, as I've done in **Figure 7-19**.

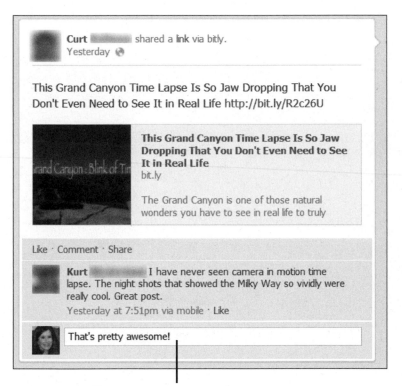

Type your comment here.

Figure 7-19

2. Type your comment in the Write a Comment box and hit
the return key when you're finished. Your response will
be posted below your friend's posting for all to see.

Post a Note

1. Notes on Facebook are like mini-blog posts. They're displayed on the Notes tab of your Timeline page. Posting a note is, in essence, posting an open letter to all your Facebook friends. You can access your notes by clicking the Notes tab on your Timeline page or by clicking the down arrow next to your Likes box and then click on Notes in the new boxes that appear.

2. You arrive at a Write a Note page, which provides you with a template to write your note. Fill in the note's title and body in the Title and Body boxes, and your note is essentially ready to be posted.

3. You may tag friends in your note by listing them in the box at the right. That way they receive a message from Facebook, inviting them to read the note — a very helpful tool if you want multiple individuals to be notified of the posting. If you don't tag anyone in your note but still want your friends to know about it, you can notify your friends by posting the note to your wall.

4. As with private messages, you have the option to attach photos, videos, and links.

 Before you publish the note to Facebook, you can set the Note's degree of privacy. Making an adjustment here (as in **Figure 7-20**) allows you to decide who can view the note: just your friends, everyone, friends of friends, or people you specify in a customized setting.

5. After you complete your note, you may preview, save draft, discard, or publish it. To publish, click the Publish button at the bottom of the page.

Privacy: ⊕ Public ▾

   ✓ ⊕ **Public**

   👥 Friends

   👥 Friends except Acquaintances   Discard

   🔒 Only Me

Facebook © 2012 · English (US   ⚙ Custom

   ⭐ Close Friends

Figure 7-20

Remove Messages from Your Wall

1. There may be a time when someone posts a message on your wall that might be too personal, or you don't want others to see. Facebook gives you the option to delete the post. (Your friend may never know that's happened unless he or she comes back to your Timeline page.) To delete a post, find the post on your Timeline page. Move your cursor over the right side of the post and a star and pencil icon appear, as shown in **Figure 7-21**.

2. When you click the pencil icon, a window opens and asks *Are you sure you want to delete this post?* If you're sure, click the Delete button and the post will be removed from your wall. Nobody will be the wiser.

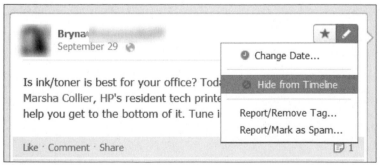

Figure 7-21

Adding Photos and Videos to Facebook

Since Facebook is all about sharing, it's up to you to share! Putting up photos of you, your family (that includes pets), and your friends is fun — and it gives your Facebook friends a chance to interact with you.

I figure you've uploaded a picture for your profile image already, but what I'm talking about in this chapter is setting up online photo albums.

So let's get started!

Get ready to ...

➡ Upload a Photo to Your Account.................... 137

➡ Create a Photo Album 141

➡ Tag Photos 146

➡ Untag Yourself in a Photo ... 149

➡ Delete a Photo 150

➡ Upload a Video to Facebook 150

Upload a Photo to Your Account

1. As with most Facebook tasks, you have more than one way to post a photo. The easiest and best way to post a *single* photo is to post it directly to your Timeline page. Start by signing in to your Facebook account and navigating to your Timeline page (click on your name in the upper-right corner).

2. Type a message about the photo in the Wall posting box that says *What's on your mind?*

3. Above your message, find the icon for uploading a photo (it looks like a little stack of photo prints) with the word Photo, as I've done in **Figure 8-1**. Clicking that icon changes the window.

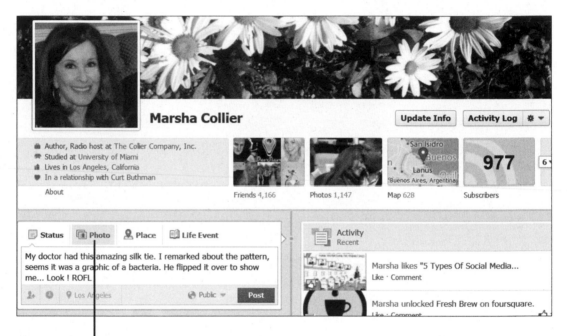

Click here to add photos

Figure 8-1

4. The new window gives you three choices: Attach Photo/Video from your computer, Use Webcam to take a photo, or Create Photo Album with many photos. Here's how those choices work:

1. *To use a photo already on your computer, click the Attach Photo/Video link.* Your window changes to a window like the one shown in **Figure 8-2**, with a browse button to select a photo from your computer's hard drive. Click Browse and a dialog box opens; from here, you can look for a photo on your computer's hard drive. Find the photo you want to upload and double-click it to select it. Click Open. The photo opens and uploads while the dialog box closes, and you see the location of your photo in the text box next to Browse. To post the photo, click Post.

📝 Status   📷 Photo   👤 Place   📖 Life Event

My doctor had this amazing silk tie. I remarked about the pattern, seems it was a graphic of a bacteria. He flipped it over to show me... Look ! ROFL

Select an image or video file on your computer.

Browse...

🌐 Public ▼   Post

Figure 8-2

 Before clicking Post when you're uploading photos to Facebook, you may wish to change your default privacy settings. **Figure 8-3** shows the options that appear when you click the arrow in the box next to the Post button. Click the appropriate privacy option, and then click Post.

Figure 8-3

2. *If you have a webcam, click Use Webcam.* If you're using a laptop computer, the webcam is most likely built in at the top of your screen. Clicking this option activates your camera automatically — and a warning appears (as shown in **Figure** 8-4). You must give the Adobe Flash Player permission to access your camera. Click the Allow radio button and your camera will have permission for this one time. You'll see yourself in the camera — smile! Or hide behind your cat (see **Figure** 8-5) if you want a cat picture, and click the small camera icon at the bottom of the screen. After selecting your privacy setting (I allow everyone to see) click Share.

Adobe Flash Player Settings

Privacy

Allow www.facebook.com to access your camera and microphone?

○ ✓ Allow   ⦿ ⊖ Deny
☐ Remember   Advanced...

Close

Figure 8-4

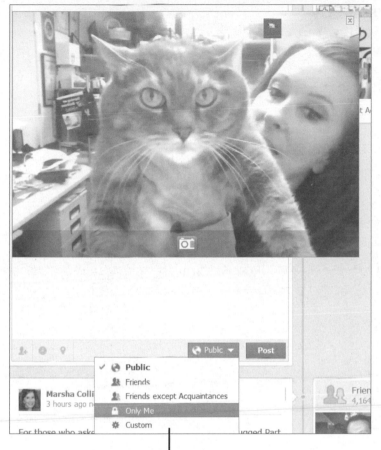

Choose who can see your photo.

Figure 8-5

>   3. *If you're ready to work with a batch of photos on Facebook,
>   click Create an Album.* I discuss this fairly complex task
>   in the next section.

Create a Photo Album

>   *1.* Facebook has many ways to get to the page where you
>   can create photo albums. Here are the two easiest:

1. *Select the Photos box on your Timeline page.* The resulting page, as shown in **Figure 8-6**, brings you to all the photos of you that you currently have on Facebook. At the top right, click the *Albums* link, and you arrive at the Create Album page.

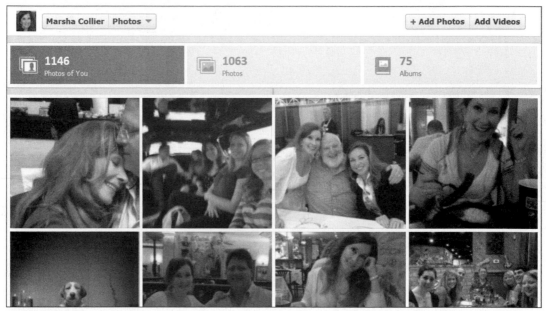

Figure 8-6

2. *Go to your Home page and, in the update box at the top of the center column, click Attach Photo / Video (as I've done in **Figure 8-7**).*

2. Click the link to Select Photos. A window opens, showing you the contents of your computer. You can navigate around your computer by clicking the folders to find where your photos reside.

3. After you find the proper folder, you can begin selecting photos for your album. If you want to select just a few, click the check boxes for individual thumbnails, one at a time, to select them for upload.

Click here to add photos.

Figure 8-7

You do not have to select all the photos just now, you can go back and add one by one by clicking *Add More Photos*.

4. After you've finished picking the images, click Open. This brings you back to the Untitled Album page (see **Figure 8-8**).

5. On the Untitled Album page, give your album a title, add comments about the album, type in the location where the photos were taken in the *Where were these taken?* box and add the date.

6. Below the description area of each photo, type a description for individual photos. If you wish, type a description in the text box, select a date, and tag friends who appear in the photos (more on tagging later). You may also set an individual privacy setting for a photo which will override the default setting.

7. Before clicking Post photos, you may select a general
default privacy setting (for who can see the album) for
the entire album.

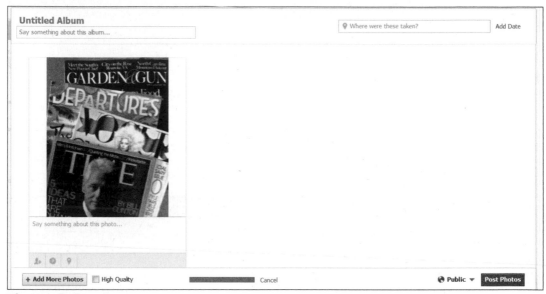

Figure 8-8

8. You can edit the album by going to your Timeline and
clicking the Photos box, then Albums. Scroll down the
page and you'll see your album (or albums), as in
Figure 8-9.

9. Click the album you want to edit and you'll be brought to
a page with thumbnail versions of your pictures. Click
Edit in the upper-right corner and you'll be brought to the
Edit page. **Figure 8-10** shows you the Edit Album page.
Go through the photos, tag the pictures, write captions
and delete any you would rather not use. When you're
done, go to the bottom of the page, and click Done.

10. Your photos will now show up on your Timeline page; if
you've tagged friends in the photos, those pictures appear
on your friends' Timeline pages.

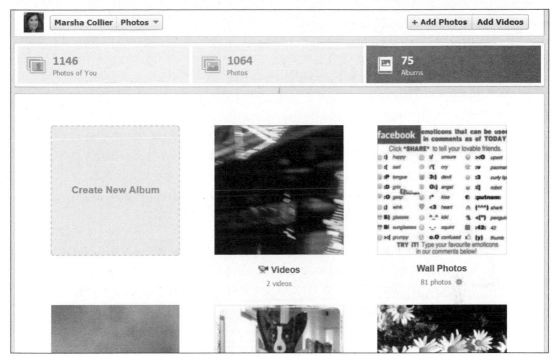

Figure 8-9

Delete a photo

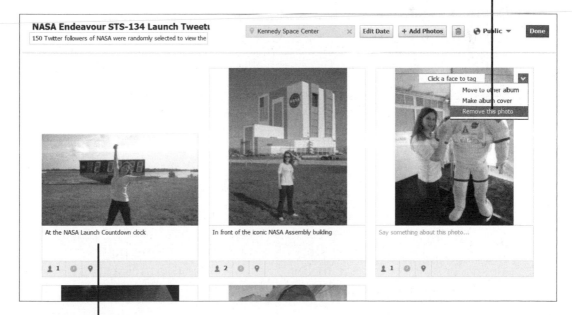

Add captions here.

Figure 8-10

Tag Photos

1. No matter where you find photos of you or one of your friends on Facebook, you'll be able to tag them. *Tagging* is the Facebook phrase for adding the names of friends to photo information. Tagging a friend makes his or her name appear when someone puts a mouse pointer over the tagged friend's image. Tagging also links the photo to the appropriate profile. Whenever friends are tagged in a photo, that photo appears on their individual walls and becomes a permanent part of their Photos areas.

 When you or anyone on Facebook is tagged, the *tagee* receives an e-mail notifying him or her of the new-found fame. Then the tagee can get online and look at the picture.

2. When you see a photo of you or one of your friends on Facebook, click it and you arrive at the Photos page. If no one has been tagged in the picture, no linkable names will appear beside it.

3. On the right, next to the photo, click the Tag Photo box, shown in **Figure 8-11**. After you have clicked this box, the text changes to Done Tagging.

4. Move your cursor, and click it on the face of one of your friends. A box will come up, framing the face.

5. Start typing your friend's name (or your name if the photo is of you), and a list of your friends pops up. Facebook narrows the selection as you type. I'm search-ing for my friend's name in **Figure 8-12**).

6. When you've found the person in the photo, click on his or her name; then bingo! The name of the person you tagged is now part of the photo — and the photo has been posted to your tagged friend's Timeline page.

Click this to add your friends to a photo.

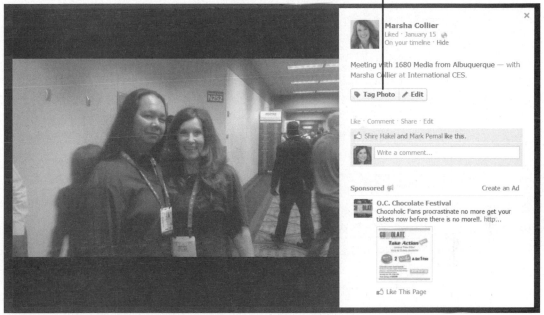

Figure 8-11

Begin typing a friend's name, and a list of your friends pops up.

Figure 8-12

7. If you have more than one friend in the picture, repeat Steps 1–5 given here until you've tagged everyone. When you've tagged all the friends in the picture, click the Done Tagging button above the picture.

 You must be friends with someone on Facebook in order to tag him or her in a photo. If you see a photo with a person you know — but aren't Facebook friends with (yet) — send that person a Friend invitation. After your friend accepts, you can then add a tag to the photo.

8. As people view the photo, they'll see the tagged names. If they move their mouse pointers over the picture, the person's name pops up (as in **Figure 8-13**).

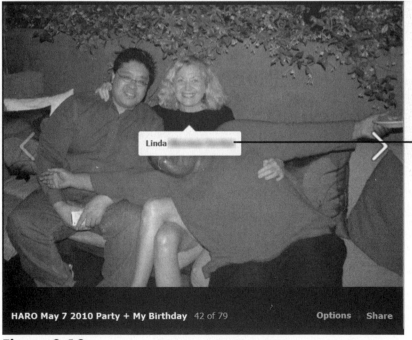

Names pop up in a tagged picutre.

HARO May 7 2010 Party + My Birthday 42 of 79   Options | Share

Linda

Figure 8-13

Untag Yourself in a Photo

1. You may get an e-mail and find that one of your friends has tagged you in a photo on Facebook. Excited, you log on to your Timeline page . . . and groan. Have no fear. If you find a photo that a friend has taken of you that doesn't quite meet your standards, you can do something about it. Click the photo, and Facebook takes you to the photo's page. Below the photo, (as in **Figure 8-14**), is an Options link.

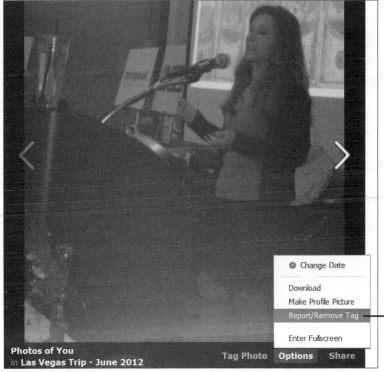

Click here to untag a picture, if you want.

Figure 8-14

2. Click Options, and the Remove/Report Tag link appears. Facebook will ask if you wish to Remove or report the tag. Click remove and the photo goes into the Facebook ether and will never be associated with your profile again. The photo does remain in your friend's album, but someone would have to view the album to see you. Once you've untagged yourself in a photo, no one but you can tag you in that particular photo again.

 If you've accidentally tagged the wrong person in a photo, you can undo your error by clicking the Remove Tag link.

Delete a Photo

1. If you upload a photo by mistake — or simply decide you'd rather not put that photo-taken-with-your-ex online — you can remove it. You can delete only the photos that you, personally, have uploaded.

 If you want to disassociate yourself from a photo that someone else uploaded, you'll have to settle for untagging yourself (see the previous task in this chapter).

2. Under the photo, on the photo page, you'll find a link to Options, as shown in **Figure 8-15**. Click it, then the Delete This Photo link, and (poof) the photo is gone from your Facebook page.

Upload a Video to Facebook

1. This isn't rocket science. If you've uploaded a photo, you can upload a video. Go to your Timeline page and click the Photos box below your cover photo.

2. Your posted photos of your friends appear on the resulting page. When you're through admiring them, look at the top right, and next to the Add Photos button, you should see an Add Videos button, as shown in **Figure 8-16**.

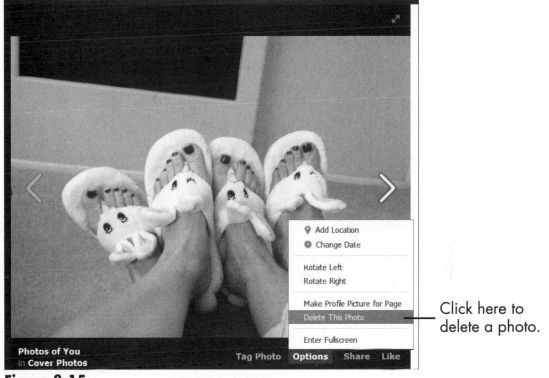

Click here to delete a photo.

Figure 8-15

Figure 8-16

3. Click the button, and you arrive at the Create a New Video page. This page, shown in **Figure 8-17**, works similarly to the Upload a Photo page. The difference is that when you click the Browse button, a standard search window opens on your computer.

Click here to browse for a video.

Create a New Video

| File Upload | Mobile Video | Record Video | Back to My Videos |

Select a video file on your computer.

[   ] Browse...

Please upload a file only if:

- The video is under **1024 MB** and under **20 minutes**.
- The video was made by you or your friends.
- You or one of your friends appears in the video.

Figure 8-17

4. Browse your computer's folders, find the video file you want to upload, and click to select it. The upload begins immediately.

5. After the upload finishes, the video will be on your Facebook page, ready for you to tag and caption.

Exploring Groups, Events, and Games

Chapter 9

*I*f you thought your teen years were a busy time, just wait. Being a member of Facebook means that you're about to have a whole new group of friends to combine with your old ones. Best of all? You'll meet people who have interests just like yours. You'll have the opportunity to attend chats and join groups — and you don't even have to get out of your pajamas.

Is there something you really like? A series of books, films, or products? Look for a related page on Facebook; many businesses are joining up on Facebook. Even California Cat Center, where I board my cats, has a Facebook page. (I visit their page to check out the cute photos of their feline guests.)

And here are some other instances of Facebook member involvement:

➥ When Kashi products stopped manufacturing my favorite shake mix, unhappy customers started a Facebook group to protest!

Get ready to . . .

➡ Find Your Favorite Things on Facebook 154

➡ Join a Facebook Group 159

➡ Start a Facebook Group 162

➡ Communicate with Group Members 167

➡ Create an Event Invitation ... 170

➡ Review Upcoming Events ... 172

➡ Export an Event to Another Calendar 173

➡ Have Some Fun with Games and Applications 174

➡ Browse Facebook Apps and Games 176

➡ Someone came up with the idea that Betty White should host *Saturday Night Live* and started a Facebook group. They had a great idea. After spreading the word through wall posts and messages, over 500,000 people joined. Eighty-eight-year-old Betty hosted the 2010 Mother's Day show, and SNL had the highest ratings in over 18 months! All because of a Facebook group.

Other ways to enjoy community action are to play games and use Facebook applications (or *apps*). To many members, these are the best parts of Facebook. Be advised: Games and other apps can burn a lot of time, but they are a lot of fun. And they're social — you can involve your online friends in your game.

So what are you waiting for? Check out the info in this chapter and get active with a Facebook group, game, or app — you can even start your own group or plan an event!

Find Your Favorite Things on Facebook

1. If you're planning on navigating your way around Facebook, you're going to be up close and personal with that little search box at the top of the page. To look at some of the magic it can perform, type the *keyword* that best describes the topic you're looking for in the search box at the top of the page. Following on the idea of looking for people who love small animals, for this example, (see **Figure 9-1**), I typed *Schipperke* (my dog's breed).

Facebook finds pages with *Schipperke* in the name and puts them in a drop-down menu. As **Figure 9-1** shows, you get a few interesting hits, and the top results are shown. If you want to check out any of the results at this point, just click the name, and you're brought to that page.

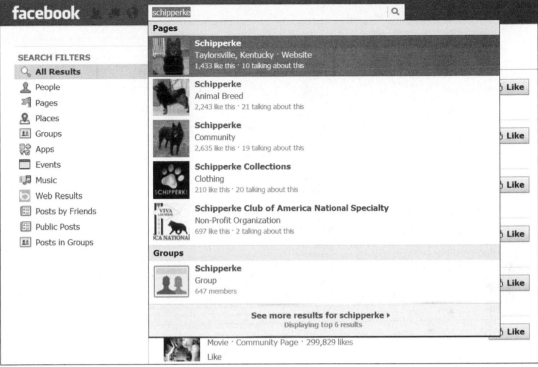

Figure 9-1

2. Click the See More Results link at the bottom of the drop-down menu. You arrive at the Facebook All Results page. As **Figure 9-2** shows, you can get some great hits — but clicking the View All Page Results link would net thousands of pages, which might be too much to browse through.

 If you look in the left on the All Results page, you see a navigation area with links to Posts by Friends, Web Results, Public Posts and Posts in Groups that also include your search term.

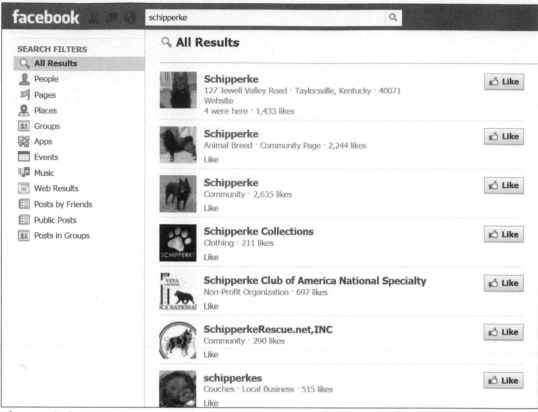

Figure 9-2

3. In the left navigation area, click Pages. Facebook takes you to a page with results consisting of pages and communities started by people who have interests in the subject. Next to each page listing is a Like link on the far right (see **Figure** 9-3). Don't jump willy-nilly into just any group that has a nice title and a cute picture. Click the title of a page and check it out before you choose to join; that way, you see what the page is really all about and who's behind it. (I clicked a couple in the example just given, and they weren't my cup of tea at all.)

SEARCH FILTERS
- Q All Results
- ⚫ People
- ▣ **Pages**
- ⚫ Places
- ⚏ Groups
- ⚏ Apps
- ▦ Events
- ⅃♫ Music
- ◉ Web Results
- ▣ Posts by Friends
- ▣ Public Posts
- ⚏ Posts in Groups

▣ **Pages**

Schipperke
127 Jewell Valley Road · Taylorsville, Kentucky · 40071
Website
4 were here · 1,433 likes   ⎙ Like

Schipperke
Animal Breed · Community Page · 2,243 likes
Like   ⎙ Like

Schipperke
Community · 2,635 likes
Like   ⎙ Like

Schipperke Collections
Clothing · 210 likes
Like   ⎙ Like

Schipperke Club of America National Specialty
Non-Profit Organization · 697 likes
Like   ⎙ Like

SchipperkeRescue.net,INC
Community · 290 likes
Like   ⎙ Like

schipperkes   ⎙ Like

Figure 9-3

4. Notice also on the left is a link to Places. Clicking on
Places brings you to Brick and Mortar business locations in
my area who have keyword matching pages on Facebook.
I changed my search to pizza (because I'm hungry) and
got pared-down results, as shown in **Figure 9-4,** maybe it's
time for lunch.

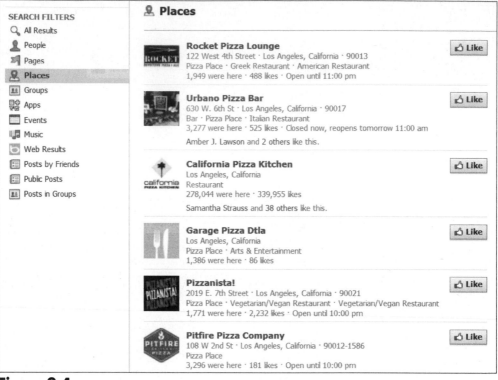

SEARCH FILTERS
- 🔍 All Results
- 👤 People
- 📄 Pages
- 👥 Places
- 👥 Groups
- Apps
- 📅 Events
- 🎵 Music
- 🌐 Web Results
- Posts by Friends
- Public Posts
- Posts in Groups

👥 **Places**

Rocket Pizza Lounge   👍 Like
122 West 4th Street · Los Angeles, California · 90013
Pizza Place · Greek Restaurant · American Restaurant
1,949 were here · 488 likes · Open until 11:00 pm

Urbano Pizza Bar   👍 Like
630 W. 6th St · Los Angeles, California · 90017
Bar · Pizza Place · Italian Restaurant
3,277 were here · 525 likes · Closed now, reopens tomorrow 11:00 am
Amber J. Lawson and 2 others like this.

California Pizza Kitchen   👍 Like
Los Angeles, California
Restaurant
278,044 were here · 339,955 likes
Samantha Strauss and 38 others like this.

Garage Pizza Dtla   👍 Like
Los Angeles, California
Pizza Place · Arts & Entertainment
1,386 were here · 86 likes

Pizzanista!   👍 Like
2019 E. 7th Street · Los Angeles, California · 90021
Pizza Place · Vegetarian/Vegan Restaurant · Vegetarian/Vegan Restaurant
1,771 were here · 2,232 likes · Open until 10:00 pm

Pitfire Pizza Company   👍 Like
108 W 2nd St · Los Angeles, California · 90012-1586
Pizza Place
3,296 were here · 181 likes · Open until 10:00 pm

Figure 9-4

5. My search is to find to find a veterinarian. Clicking on a link in the resulting list takes you to the page. In **Figure 9-5,** you can see I clicked on a charming page from a veterinarian. After reviewing the page, I clicked Like and became a fan.

 If you'd rather just not look at the top results, but don't want to trudge through thousands; add another keyword in your search terms. Typing another keyword in the box can help you refine your search. Also, you can click each link in the left navigation area to further narrow your results.

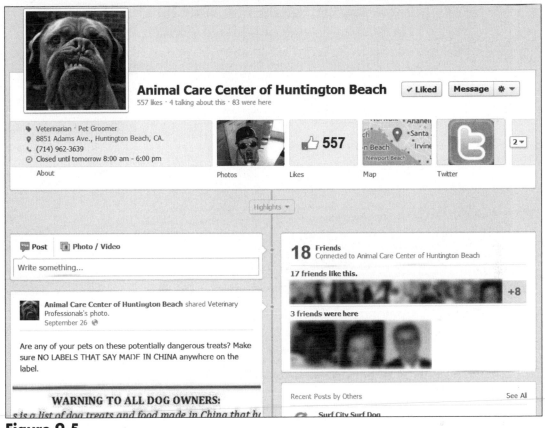

Figure 9-5

Join a Facebook Group

As a member of Facebook, you'll no doubt want to connect with people who have common likes — and doing that through groups is quick and easy! Here's how:

1. Find a group through search. To find a group you are interested in, you can search for your keywords as I describe in the preceding section. Then just click the Groups link on the left after you receive your search results.

Click a group title that suits your fancy and check it out. If you think you've found one that you'd like to join, click the Join Group link on the top of the group's page.

In **Figure 9-6,** you can see the link. After looking at many pages, I could see this was one I liked enough that it was worth joining.

To join the group, click here.

Figure 9-6

 Some Facebook groups are Closed (private). In this case, you need to click the Join Group link on the Group page and await confirmation. Confirmation will come to your through e-mail and Facebook messages. Some groups require an invitation in order to join. The only way you will be able to join these groups is if a group administrator invites you and gives you access.

2. Your friends may add you to a Group of which they are a member (or have just started). You will receive a notification that shows up in the Notifications area (globe icon) in the top navigation bar, and the Group will show up in a list, as in **Figure 9-7)** in the Groups link found on the left side of your home page.

Click here . . .   See group requests here.

Marsha Collier

Groups   + Create Group

FAVORITES
📰 News Feed
💬 Messages   99+
📅 Events   20+

ADS
🅕 Ads Manager

PAGES
Marsha Collier   6
Computer and Technology ...
👍 Like Pages

GROUPS
💀 Happy Hour Mafia
THRIFTING-WITH-...   20+
Peaks Island Sea Salt & Tr...
Chain of Daisies   3
Working eBay - Tips...   20+

✏ 💀 Happy Hour Mafia		Used today
✏ 💬 The Perils of Cyber-Dating		Used today
✏ 🍾 Family Group		Used today
✏ 👤 STS-134 NASATweetup		Used today
✏ ✊ Interrobang ?		Used today
✏ 🥤 SoMe Friends		Used today
✏ 🌐 Progressive eBay Strategy		Used today
✏ 👤 NASATweetup Alumni		Used today
✏ eBay Radio Party & Conference		Used today
✏ Peaks Island Sea Salt & Trading Co		Used today

Figure 9-7

3. If, after you visit the page, you find the group isn't something you are interested in participating in — no sweat. You can remove yourself quietly. So (say) you're really not a morning person and don't want to join your neighbor's "Good Morning Coffee" group, you can always say you never saw the group. You can also manually remove yourself.

- Go to the Group page. On the top of the page (next to Notifications) you will see a small cog signifying settings. Click there and the drop-down menu shown in **Figure** 9-8 appears.

- Click Leave Group and a window pops up to confirm you wish to leave the group. The action of leaving a Group prevents members from re-adding you. Should you wish to rejoin, you will have to visit the group page and click Join Group. If at this point you are sure you want to leave, click Leave Group.

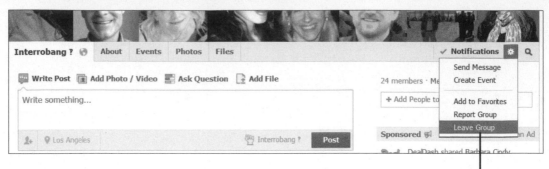

Click here to leave group.

Figure 9-8

Start a Facebook Group

Groups can work as a substitute for mass e-mails you might otherwise send out to your family, friends, or any group you're are a member of in the real world.

1. Want to plan a family reunion? Perhaps you might be interested in starting a new group on Facebook based on your hobby? You can do it. Start by clicking the Groups link found in the navigation bar on the left side of your home page. (You may have to click the More link first.) You'll be brought to your Groups page.

 If you'd like, you can set up your Group so that you get an automatic e-mail any time a member posts a comment or status update.

2. Click the Create Group button on the upper-right side of your page. A pop-up box appears with the Create Group form window.

3. Give your Group a name by typing it in the Group Name text box provided, as shown in **Figure 9-9**.

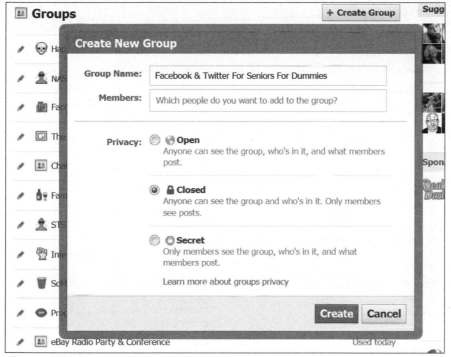

Figure 9-9

4. Add the initial members by typing their names in the Members text box. As **Figure 9-10** shows, as you type, a drop-down menu will appear, showing matching Facebook friends. After you see an entry with the correct person's name and photo, click it, and that friend becomes part of your list in the Member box. Continue to type in names until you've invited all the folks you want in the Group. Facebook will suggest new members, based on your relationships with the members you enter.

5. Click the appropriate option button next to the Privacy setting you want for your Group. There are three options shown in **Figure 9-11**:

- **Open:** Anyone who finds your group on Facebook can find it in search and join the group. Your friends can see that you've joined an open group in their news feed.

Figure 9-10

- **Closed:** The group name will appear in search. When viewing the page, its members and people invited to join the group are visible, but only members can see posts in the group.

- **Secret:** A Secret Group won't appear in search, and the only way people can join is if the administrator (or one of the members — if this option is set up) invites them. No one else will even know that a Secret Group exists.

You can change your Privacy setting later on if you wish — as long as the total membership of your Group remains under 250.

6. Click the Create Group button when you're finished.

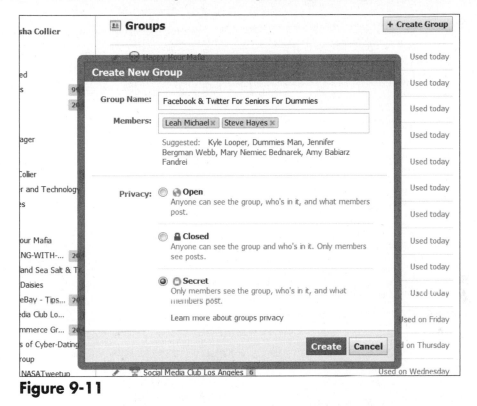

Figure 9-11

7. A new window opens, asking you to select from an assortment of fanciful icons, shown in **Figure 9-12**, to identify with your Group (the default icon is so boring, so pick something appropriate). This icon will show up on your Home page's navigation links next to the name of your Group. After you have selected your icon, click Okay and your group will be live on Facebook.

8. You will be transported to your brand-spanking-new Group Home page on Facebook, **Figure 9-13** shows my new group!

Figure 9-12

Figure 9-13

 Be aware! Facebook has a rule about groups: "Groups that attack a specific person or group of people (e.g. racist, sexist, or other hate groups) will not be tolerated. Creating such a group will result in the immediate termination of your Facebook account."

9. You can edit your page and settings at any time by clicking the little cog icon next to the word Notifications, shown in **Figure** 9-14, that appears (only to you) on the sections of your group page.

Figure 9-14

Communicate with Group Members

When you set up a group on Facebook, you are usually the group administrator (*admin*, for short) by default. Everyone else in the group are members; they can post, as shown in **Figure 9-15**, to the wall and share with the group as well. As the group administrator, you will be able to adjust the privacy settings, edit information, and add a group profile photo. It's just like setting up your own Facebook page. Think of your group page the same as your regular Profile page; it's not any different, with the following exceptions:

➠ If you're the admin of your group (the Big Kahuna, the person who created the group and runs it), you decide who can join the group, and ban or remove any member who does not play well with others.

➠ A very handy feature of Groups is that you can share files with other members of the group. You can upload files from your computer, or from those hosted on Dropbox.com, the file storage and sharing site. If you make changes to a file, all group members will get an update.

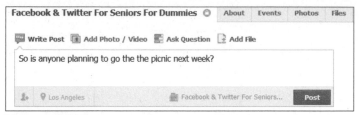

Figure 9-15

But the magic of groups is that admins can send blanket communications to all members. Below the group photo is an area of links where Facebook allows you unique controls. (Only the admins can see these.)

➡ **Message All Members.** Clicking this link will take you to a page that looks like any other Facebook message page. The only difference is that when you click *Send*, the message will go to all the members of your Group.

➡ **Promote Group with Ad.** If you'd like to buy a Facebook ad to promote your group, here's your chance!

➡ **Edit Group Settings.** This takes you to an Administration page where you decide about privacy settings, page setup, and general information.

➡ **Edit Members.** This takes you to a Member Administration page where you can view all your members and choose officers or other admins. **Figure 9-16** shows you the available tabs and options.

Facebook & Twitter For Seniors For Dummies | About | Events | Photos | Files | ✓ Notifications ⚙

Write Post | Add Photo / Video | Ask Question | Add File

Write something...

Marsha Collier created the group.
Like · Comment · Unfollow Post · 18 hours ago

3 members (2
+ Add People

What should
Add a Descript

Send Message
Create Event

Add to Favorites
Edit Group Settings
Report Group
Leave Group

Figure 9-16

➠ **Set up a Group e-mail address.** Perhaps some group members rarely visit the Facebook site. By setting up a group exclusive e-mail address, members can send posts via e-mail to appear on the wall.

➠ **Create Group Event.** Want to have a meeting? A party? Admins only can click here and go to the Create an Event page. **Figure 9-17** shows you how this procedure differs from a regular Facebook event invitation. You have three options:

a. *Public:* Anyone can see this Event and its information. Anyone can RSVP or invite others to this Event.

b. *Friends:* Anyone can see this Event, but its content is only shown to guests. People need to be invited or request invitations to be able to RSVP.

c. *Invite Only:* Only people who are invited can see this Event and details. People will need to be invited and to RSVP.

Create New Event for Facebook & Twitter For Seniors...

Name	New Edition Pizza Party!
Details	Celebrate this chapter of the Facebook & Twitter For Seniors updated edition
Where	📍 Google Plus ✕
When	10/15/2012 📅 8:00 pm PDT End time?
Privacy	🏢 Facebook & Twitter For Seniors For Dummies

- 🌐 Public
- 👥 Friends
- ✉ Invite Only

✓ 🏢 **Facebook & Twitter For Seniors For Dummies**

☑ Invit ...   Cancel

Figure 9-17

Create an Event Invitation

1. Are you planning a party? Facebook is a good way to send out invitations. Any Facebook member can create an event and invite all their friends. Start by going to your Facebook Home page and clicking the Events tab found in the toolbar on the left side of the screen (as in **Figure 9-18**). In the upper-right corner of your Events page, you'll see the Create Event button.

2. Clicking the Create Event button takes you to the Create Event page. Fill out the when, what, and where of the event and decide if you want the event to be Public, for Friends or Invite Only.

3. Click Invite Friends to prepare your guest list from your Facebook friends list (as shown in **Figure 9-19**) by placing a check in the box next to your friend's name and photo. When you're through selecting folks, click Save. Decide if invitees can invite others and whether the Event page should show the guest list. When you're sure the invitation is correct, click Create.

Click this button to go to the Create Event page.

Figure 9-18

Figure 9-19

4. After clicking Create, you will be brought to the Event page (mine is shown in **Figure 9-20**) where you can upload a photo to doll up the page. Your event, if Public, will appear on Facebook and invitations will be sent to the friends you selected.

 As the event administrator, you can adjust the event's privacy settings, invite more people, edit the guest list, cancel the event, edit the event, and send messages to your guests

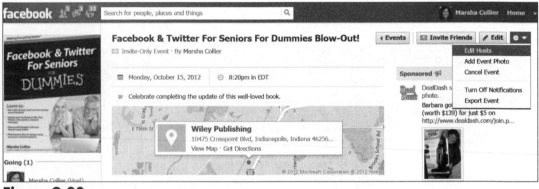

Figure 9-20

Review Upcoming Events

1. To review your upcoming events, click the Events link in the links on the left side of your homepage. You're taken to your Events page, where you can view all your upcoming events in chronological order. Next to the word Events at the top of the page, you can select to view the upcoming Events in a list or in a calendar format. Below the events for the current day, you will also see a list of those of your friends for whom today is their birthday — so you can post a "Happy Birthday" message to their pages.

2. Your events are listed on the Events page (refer to **Figure 9-18**) and you have the chance to respond to the invitations right there. I always recommend that you take a moment and click the title of the event so you can find out exactly what's planned and where the event is. If you know all those details and are in a hurry, you can click the Join button below the event. By clicking on the event title, you can go to the page and write a short note to go along with your RSVP.

3. The best laid plans often change and can also change your mind at any time (assuming it's okay with the host). Change your RSVP on the Event page, by clicking your RSVP and selecting from the drop-down menu shown in **Figure 9-21**.

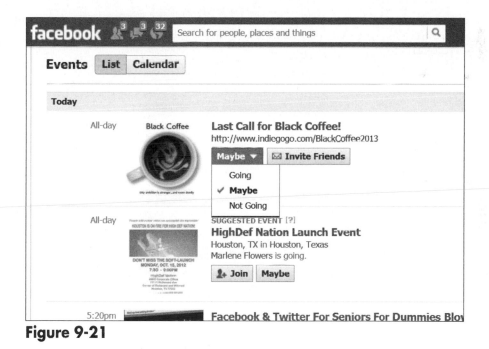

Figure 9-21

Export an Event to Another Calendar

1. If you don't rely on Facebook as your main event calendar, it's a good idea to use the Export feature to send your Facebook Events into whatever calendar you use. Facebook supports lots of applications, including

Microsoft Outlook and Apple iCal. Facebook also claims that it can export to Google Calendar, but I've never been able to make that feature work consistently.

 Your Events section shows you all the events you've been invited to. Rather than merely clicking the Respond button, click the event's title to see all the details.

2. When you're on the Event invitation page, you can export the event by clicking the Export Event link — found by clicking the arrow next to the cog icon on the right side of the Event page — and selecting Export Event. A pop-up window will appear (as shown in **Figure 9-22**), giving you the option to save to your calendar, or send yourself an e-mail with the event details.

Export Event

◉ Save to calendar

○ Send to email   talk2marsha@coolebaytools.com ▾

Subscribe to all upcoming events on your calendar:

webcal://www.facebook.com/ical/u.php?uid=757434664&key=AQAKBvy-08o2IyyH

[Export] [Cancel]

Figure 9-22

Have Some Fun with Games and Applications

Your first exposure to Facebook's games or applications (apps) happens when you see requests from some of your friends in your notifications or on your Home page like those shown in **Figure 9-23**. Facebook has loads of games and applications. Applications are a little different from games, since they don't require as many hours to have fun with them.

Words With Friends
★★★★★

Games, Word Game | Jeff Long, John Lawson and 232 other friends play this

Play Game **Send to Mobile**

By clicking "Play Game" or "Send to Mobile" above, this app will receive:

- Your basic info [?]
- Your email address (marsha.collier@gmail.com)

The #1 mobile word game Words With Friends Free is available for Facebook, iPhone, iPad, iPod touch, and Android. Experience for yourself why millions of players are addicted to the word building, triple score seeking, chat bubble sending goodness of Words With Friends.

This app may post on your behalf, including achievements you earned, words you played and more.

Who can see posts this app makes for you on your Facebook timeline: [?]

PRAISE FOR WORDS WITH FRIENDS

👥 Friends ▼

- "Delightfully addictive." – GeekSugar

- "Social gaming at its finest." – Fox News

By proceeding, you agree to Words With Friends's Terms of Service and Privacy Policy

- "The premise of 'Words' is simple: you fire it up and are playing a Scrabble-like word game against one of your friends in seconds." – TechCrunch

Visit App Page
Share
Block

WORDS WITH FRIENDS ADDICTIVE FEATURES

- Simple and familiar crossword gameplay you know and love

- Turn-based design lets you play up to 20 games simultaneously

Figure 9-23

Facebook's many applications enable you to do almost anything you can imagine — send gifts, take quizzes, throw snowballs — you name it! A popular type of app centers around taking quizzes. You can find a quiz on everything from how to determine "What Sex and the City character you are" to "Which color best suits your personality." Another very popular application lets you make up your own quizzes to send to your friends.

🎯 Playing with a quiz application lets your friends see that you have taken the quiz by posting your results to your news feed. Potentially, your friends will play along with you.

The most popular games on Facebook are currently the products of Zynga, the creators of Words With Friends, Farmville, Mafia Wars, ChefVille, Texas HoldEm Poker, and numerous other games. When you find a game (or an application) you'd like to participate in, you must give permission for Facebook to allow the game to have access to your account, by clicking Play Game or Send to Mobile as shown in **Figure 9-23**. You must agree with specific terms for each game, and these terms will be posted under the acceptance buttons. If you want to play, this access is a requirement. So stick to the most popular, time tested games.

Browse Facebook Apps and Games

1. To browse apps on Facebook, go to your home page and click the link to the App Center in the toolbar on the left. To see which apps you are using (if you've signed up for any), click the Apps heading just above the Apps Center.

2. To see all the available applications, you simply browse Facebook's Applications Directory. But finding this directory through a Facebook search is a little tricky, so just type **www.facebook.com/appcenter** in your browser's address bar. Press Enter, and you see a page similar to the one shown in **Figure 9-24**. Click the words Game Feed in the left side toolbar, and you see a page similar to the one in **Figure 9-25** showing your friend's recent Apps and Game activity.

3. The resulting App Center has a number of category links on the left side toolbar. By clicking these links you will find specific types of applications, for example, Games and Utilities. Click a link, and you see featured items and application recommendations in that category. Browse through and you'll be sure to find an application to suit your needs.

4. To specifically find games for Mobile devices, click the Mobile box at the top of the left toolbar, as shown in **Figure 9-26**. You'll see New, Top and Trending apps for mobile gaming. Click the blue Go To Application button on the left side of the page under the large game icon.

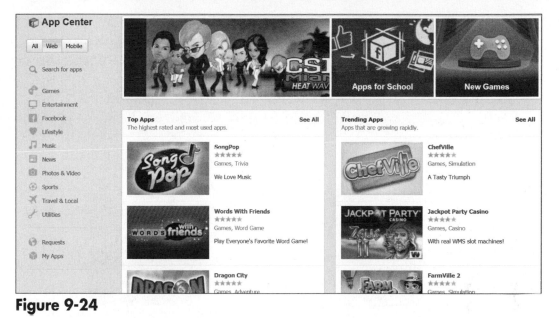

Figure 9-24

Apps and Games
Your friends' recent apps and games activity

Jay ▇▇▇▇▇ got a new high score in SongPop.

SongPop
New Score: 18,776 points
Old Score: 16,075 points

Like · Comment · Share · Play Now · October 4 at 9:50am · 🌐

Write a comment...

Jay ▇▇▇▇▇ earned an achievement in SongPop.

Speedster: I
Guess each song in a challenge correctly - in 3 seconds or less!

Like · Comment · Share · Play Now · October 4 at 9:50am · 🌐

Ruby ▇▇▇▇ reached a level on Bubble Blitz.

Level 37
Level up to unlock new features and powers.
XP Required: **62900**

Figure 9-25

To find games for mobile devices, click here.

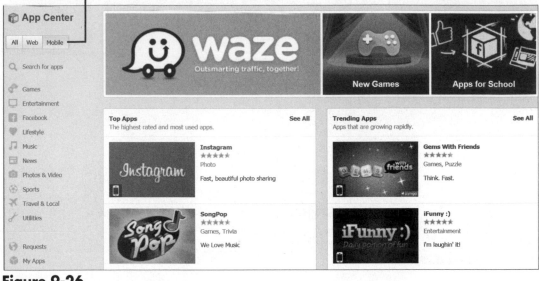

Figure 9-26

Currently, millions of people play these top games:

➡ **Farmville 2:** 6,900,000 daily active players. Ever wanted to have a farm? Now you can without getting your hands dirty! Farmville 2, the sequel to the still-popular Farmville allows you to build and cultivate your own. The game comes complete with your own plot of land and lots of opportunities to grow your farm through planting, harvesting, gifting, and building.

➡ **Texas HoldEm Poker:** 6,900,000 daily active players. Fancy yourself a poker star? This is the top poker game in the world. Play online with your friends and see who's got the best poker face, or meet some new people. The game also runs weekly tournaments. (By the way, your winnings are virtual — no cash payouts.)

➡ **Words With friends:** 6,100,000 daily active players. Play familiar crossword games with friends or randomly selected opponents. On Treasure Isle, you visit strange places, dig for rare and valuable treasure with your friends, and decorate your very own island.

➡ **ChefVille:** 7,200,000 daily active players. Become a restaurateur and run your own restaurant. Choose your menu from dozens of dishes to cook, then slice, chop, sauté, and bake your way to success. You can decorate your Café and hire friends.

➡ **Mafia Wars:** 20,000,000 players. Did you love Al Pacino in The Godfather? You might just have fun playing Mafia Wars, the wildly popular crime game. Build alliances, amass property, and fight mobs of enemies in games of power and deception.

Part III

And Now, It's Twitter Time

The 5th Wave   By Rich Tennant

"I'd respond to this person's comment on Twitter, but I'm a former Marine, Bernard, and a Marine never retweets."

A Beginner's Guide to Twitter

Chapter 10

1 really enjoy the time I spend on Twitter. I can visit the site at any hour and find a friend to chat with. It may not be someone I've met in real life, but someone I've met on Twitter with whom I have fun. People on Twitter come from all walks of life, and you can make friends with people of all ages.

Keep in mind that Twitter is not just about posting pithy thoughts online; it's all about having conversations. The second-best part of Twitter is that by listening (reading other people's posts, or *Tweets*, as they're nick-named), you learn all sorts of interesting things. Most news events appear on Twitter before you hear about them on radio or television.

Twitter users love to spread information of all sorts. When you find your niche, you'll see what fun participating on the site can be.

Your posts on Twitter are limited to 140 characters. (When you send text messages on your phone, you're allowed 160 characters.) Figuring out how to abbreviate your thoughts and get your message into such a short sentence will definitely exercise your brain; it can take a bit of thinking!

Get ready to . . .

➡ Register with Twitter 184

➡ Find People to Follow 188

➡ Adjust Your Account
   Settings 194

➡ Upload Your Avatar 197

➡ Select a Theme for
   Your Profile Page 199

➡ Set Up Notices 200

➡ Know Twitter Shorthand 201

In this chapter, I help you get started with Twitter — by registering, setting up an account and profile page, deciding what notices you want to receive, and getting familiar with Twitter shorthand. Are you ready? Let's sign up and start making new friends!

Register with Twitter

1. As with all interactive Web sites, you can't play until you sign up and agree to the rules. So type **www.twitter.com** in your browser's address bar, press Enter, and you'll come to a page similar to the one in **Figure 10-1**.

Click here to register with Twitter.

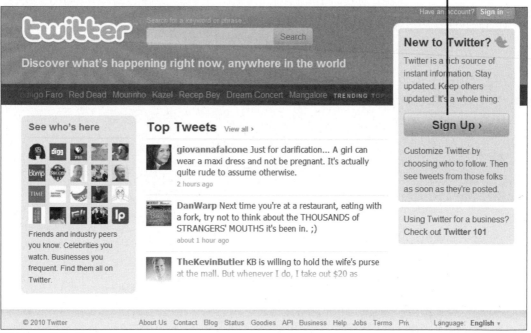

Figure 10-1

2. Before you start to click things, take a look at the Twitter Web page. You find a list of topics that are currently popular (trending) on the site. Don't worry if you aren't interested in any topics you see here. With over 75 million users, I'm sure that a few will have interests similar to yours! You also see some of the famous Twtterati who use the service (on the left), as well as a scroll of top tweets from the current timeline.

3. To start your registration, click the button that says Get Started, Join Today, or Sign Up. The greeting changes from minute to minute, but you get the drift, right? You're presented with a page prompting you to enter some information that identifies you to Twitter, as follows:

1. *Type in your full, real name so that your friends can find you if they look for you in Twitter search.* (Chapter 11 tells you more about searching on Twitter.)

2. *Come up with a catchy username for use on Twitter.*

    Your username can be a nickname or your real name, whichever you prefer. If you choose a nickname, it can be a name that reflects one of your hobbies, or a special interest you may have. Get creative! But remember: Your username cannot have any spaces or symbols, just letters and/or numbers. If your selected username is already in use on the site, Twitter will let you know, as shown in **Figure 10-2**.

3. *Select a password and type it in the Password text box.*

   Twitter will let you know the security strength of your password after you type it in.

    You may want to check out the information on picking a password in Chapter 3 to make sure you select a secure password.

4. *Type in your e-mail address.*

   This information will not be shown to anyone; Twitter uses it to send you a confirmation e-mail message and (after you're active on the site) to send you any notifications you've requested.

Fill in your information.

Figure 10-2

Click here to create your account.

4. Click to check the box labeled Let Others Find Me by My Email Address. Do this if you want your friends to be able to type your e-mail address into a Twitter search to find you. If that's an option you don't want, just uncheck it (if it's checked by default), and leave it without the check mark.

5. Read and agree to the Terms of Service. Every Web site has Terms of Service (TOS), which are basically the rules that everyone participating on the site has to follow. Read them and print them out if you want. Even if you don't do that, know that opening your account on Twitter means you agree to abide by their rules.

6. Click the Create My Account button, and you're well on your way to becoming a member of one of the largest and fastest-growing online communities. Plus, you'll be one of the cool kids who are considered "early adopters" in your group of friends (at least the tech-savvy ones)!

7. Tackle the Captcha code (the crazy looking words). Before Twitter lets you join the throng, you have to prove you aren't a robot or a computer. (Believe it or not, there are people who set up their computers to sign up automatically on sites all over the Web — weird, eh? Captcha codes are designed so only human eyes can figure them out.)

The Captcha code may be a bit difficult to read, as shown in **Figure 10-3**. If you can't read it, click the Get Two New Words link at the right to try some different words. If you can't read it after a couple of tries, click Hear a Set of Words, and the words will play on your computer's speakers. The code words are random and may not make sense. But when you've figured out the words for the Captcha test, type them in the box as prompted and click the Finish button.

If you can't read this... try another option.

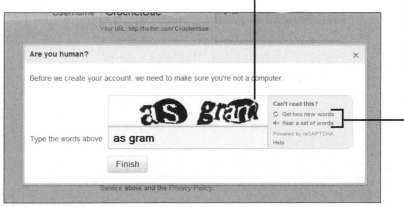

Figure 10-3

8. Clicking Finish brings you to a topic page, similar to the one shown in **Figure 10-4**. Move on to the next section, which instructs you about how to find folks to follow on Twitter.

Figure 10-4

Find People to Follow

At this point, I need to explain the workings of Twitter. For the whole experience to work, you need to find people to *follow*. These would be people you might want to hear from — your Twitter friends, your online community. You can follow or unfollow anyone at any time. When you follow someone

⇒ Each time that person posts a comment (tweet), you will see it on your Twitter home page.

⇒ The folks you follow may follow you back, and if they do, they'll see *your* comments on *their* pages.

➡ You can send a Direct Message (or DM) to someone you're following. A DM is like a text message that you send on your cell phone. It's a private message between you and the recipient. It does not appear in the public stream of tweets. In the "Set Up Notices" section later in this chapter, I show you how you can have these message sent directly to your cell phone if you desire. That way you can respond to a DM without having to go back to your computer.

 If you have to pay an additional fee for text messages on your mobile-phone plan, sending and receiving too many direct messages could get expensive. Be sure you have a full data plan on your smartphone if you want to get these messages.

1. To begin finding people to follow, click a topic that interests you from the list on the left (refer to Figure 10-4). Suggested Twitter users (or sources) will be listed to the right, as shown in **Figure 10-5**. Be sure to scroll down the page so you see the full list; you can click more at the bottom to see more.

2. If you see someone and think that you might be interested in hearing what that person has to say, follow him or her by clicking the Follow button to the right of the name.

3. Repeat Steps 1 and 2 (click another category and scroll though the names) to find more people to follow. When you feel like you have enough people selected, click the Next Step: Friends button at the bottom right.

 Know that you can always search for more people to add to your Follow list after you're fully set up on the site — so don't feel pressured to keep looking for people to follow as you're getting started.

Click a topic here...to find people to follow here.

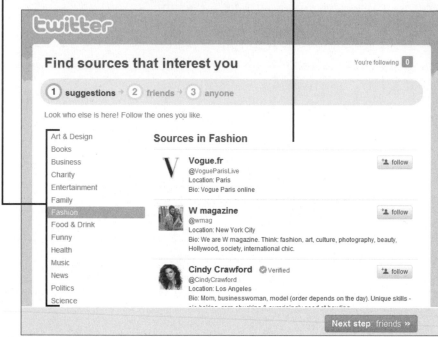

Figure 10-5

4. The next page you see, as in **Figure 10-6**, lists Web-based e-mail services Gmail, Yahoo, and AOL. You can use these to find (and follow) people from your e-mail lists who are already on Twitter. If you use one of these services and want to search Twitter for your e-mail buddies, you can click the name of the e-mail service and type your user ID and password when prompted (this is safe to do because Twitter doesn't store your password).

 Personally, I'd skip this step. You might want to be a bit more settled and secure with your participation on Twitter before you involve your real-world friends. (The point of this book is to make *you* the expert!)

Find friends on Twitter through an online service.

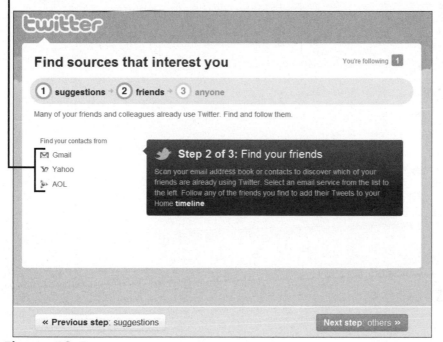

Figure 10-6

5. Click the Next Step: Others button. On the resulting page, you see an empty text box. If you have a friend who's already on Twitter, type his or her name in the text box and click Search.

If you don't know anyone to follow, just type in my name **MarshaCollier**. When my Twitter result comes up on-screen (as it does in **Figure 10-7**), click the Follow button and we'll be connected. (Don't forget to say "Hi" once we're connected — I show you how to do that in Chapter 11.)

Search for a friend's name.

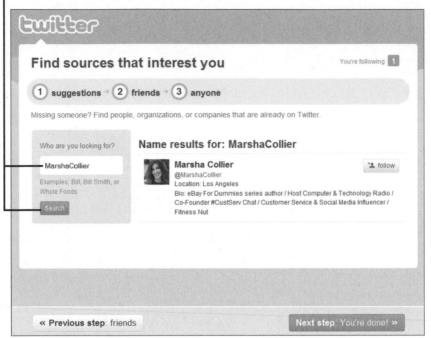

Figure 10-7

6. When you're finished typing in people's names and following them (remember, you can do this all later after you've gotten the lay of Twitter-land), click the Next step: You're Done button. You're now on your Twitter home page where you see the most recent tweets from the people you followed (check out **Figure 10-8**). If you haven't followed anyone, your page will look pretty blank.

7. While you've been doing all this following, Twitter sent an e-mail message to the e-mail address you provided when you filled out the sign-up form. Open your e-mail program and look for the message. You'll see an e-mail like the one shown in **Figure 10-9**. Click the link in the e-mail, or copy it (by highlighting the link and pressing the Ctrl+C) and paste it (by clicking in your browser's address line and pressing Ctrl+V) into your browser.

See tweets from the people you follow here.

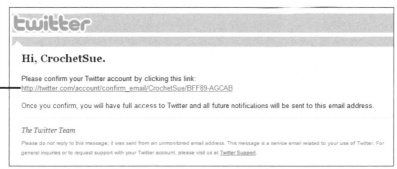

Figure 10-8

Click here to confirm your Twitter account.

Figure 10-9

You are now an official member of Twitter; congratulations!

Adjust Your Account Settings

1. Click the Settings link on the top right side of your Twitter home page. The information that you input when you signed up is filled in on this page. Scroll down so that you can add some additional important data.

 As an official member of Twitter, you'll need to let other Twitter members know who you are. People follow other people who interest them on Twitter, and identifying yourself as an interesting, charming person will add a lot to the time you spend on Twitter.

2. Choose a language. English is filled in as the default (and I assume you speak English since you're reading this book). If you'd prefer a different language, click the down arrow on the Language text box and select another language from the drop-down menu.

3. Check for your correct time zone. GMT (Greenwich Mean Time) will be filled in. If you don't live in the United Kingdom (where Greenwich is, the last I looked), I suggest that you click the down arrow and select the time zone where you live from the drop-down menu.

4. Click the Add a Location to Your Tweets check box (a check mark appears in the box) and (not surprisingly) you add the location you're tweeting from to your tweets. This is an optional setting, and you don't have to check this. By not revealing your exact location, you can maintain a semblance of privacy. (I usually don't put a check by this setting; I prefer not to reveal my exact location.)

5. If you click to check the Protect My Tweets check box, your tweets will not appear in the public Twitter timeline. Checking this option kind of defeats the purpose of Twitter; you're on the site to be part of the giant conversation.

If you protect your tweets, there's a chance that people won't follow you back when you follow them. People like to know what they're getting into when they follow someone — and if they can't see your tweets, they may be concerned that you may not be the kind of person they'd want to follow. Twitter is all about *transparency*.

6. After you fill out the balance of your account information, click Save. You'll have to retype your password to save your account settings.

If you've forgotten your password, click the Forgot Your Password link and Twitter sends you a reminder by e-mail so you can reset your password. Click the link in the e-mail message or copy the link into your browser. You arrive at a page where you can change your password, as shown in **Figure 10-10**. Type in your new password twice (the second time is to verify your typing) and click the Change button.

Type a password twice to change it.

twitter

Home Profile Find People Settings Help Sign out

Change your Twitter password
Please choose a password to use with your Twitter account

New Password: •••••••   Good

Verify New Password: •••••••

Change

A note about third-party services
If you have trusted a third-party Twitter service or software with your password and you change it here, you'll need to re-authenticate to make that software work. Never enter your password in a third-party service or software that looks suspicious.

© 2010 Twitter About Us Contact Blog Status Goodies API Business Help Jobs Terms Privacy

Figure 10-10

To change your password at any time, just click the Settings link at the top right of your Twitter home page and, on the resulting Settings page, click the Password link that appears above your settings.

7. At this point, your pals at Twitter are so revved up to have you aboard that they send you a welcoming e-mail message. **Figure 10-11** shows you a sample of what the message looks like.

---

twitter

Hello, new Twitter-er!

Here is your account information.

Your username: CrochetSue
Your profile: http://twitter.com/CrochetSue

Using Twitter is going to change the way you think about staying in touch with friends and family. Did you know you can send and receive tweets (Twitter updates) via mobile texting or the web? To do that, you'll want to visit your settings page (and you'll want to invite some friends).

Activate Phone: http://twitter.com/devices
Invite Your Friends: http://twitter.com/invite

The New York Times calls Twitter "one of the fastest-growing phenomena on the Internet." TIME Magazine says, "Twitter is on its way to becoming the next killer app," and Newsweek noted that "Suddenly, it seems as though all the world's a-twitter." What will you think? http://twitter.com

Biz Stone and The Twitter Team
http://twitter.com/biz

Please do not reply to this message; it was sent from an unmonitored email address. This message is a service email related to your use of Twitter. For general inquiries or to request support with your Twitter account, please visit us at Twitter Support.

Figure 10-11

Open your e-mail. On it, you find that Twitter notifies you of a few things:

- **Your username**. I entered *CrochetSue* as my sample username when I first signed up, and there it is!

- **The URL** (Internet address) of your Twitter profile. You can include this in your e-mails to let your friends know where they can find you on Twitter.

- **A link to activate your phone**. If you'd like to receive Twitter notifications on your smartphone, you can click this link to input your cell phone number.

Activating your phone will also allow you to send tweets from your cell phone. FYI: You text your messages to Twitter at 40404.

- **An Invite Your Friends link**. Click this link and you arrive on a page where you can type in the e-mail addresses of people you'd like to have join you on Twitter. Twitter will send them an e-mail message on your behalf, inviting them to join. I recommend that you ask your friends whether they'd like to join Twitter before you send those e-mails. Some people feel that invitation e-mails are an intrusion.

Upload Your Avatar

1. Get to your Twitter home page by browsing to www.twitter.com, signing in (if you're not already), and clicking the Home link near the top of the page. Your home page probably looks pretty darned bare before you install the bells and whistles. In the place where your photo should go is a small Twitter bird icon, which looks nothing like you! So get ready to make your page look like it belongs to a Twitter pro.

2. Click the Settings link in the toolbar at the top-right of the page and then click the Profile link on the Settings page (see **Figure 10-12**). You're now at the Profile Settings page, and your first order of business is to upload an image to serve as your avatar on Twitter.

twitter

Home Profile Find People Settings Help Sign out

MarshaCollier's settings

Account   Password   Mobile   Notices   Profile   Design   Connections

Figure 10-12

Nope, we're not revisiting James Cameron's epic 3D film *Avatar*. In tech-speak, an *avatar* is an image that represents you online. On Twitter, it means a picture of you. People want to see a picture when they go to follow someone new, so they have some idea of who they're becoming friends with. Some people use pictures of their dogs or the logos for their businesses as avatars, but if you're on Twitter to make friends, I suggest posting a flattering image of yourself.

3. To upload your photo, click the Browse button to open a dialog box where you can look for a photo on your computer.

4. In the dialog box, find the folder on your computer where you store your photos and select a photo by clicking it so that the name of the photo appears in the File Name box. Click Open after you select your picture, and you return to the Twitter Profile setup. (The photo you select can be no more than 700K in size, and can be in either jpg, gif, or png format.) The filename and location on your computer appears in the picture box. Voilá!

5. As long as you're on this page, it's time to fill in your bio. In keeping with the brevity of the site, you have 160 characters to describe yourself. You can change this description at any time, so just put in a little information about yourself for now. You can compare your bio to those of the people you meet on Twitter and refine it as you go.

6. Click Save at the bottom of the page, and your settings are saved. You return to the Profile settings page, and you see the picture you just uploaded next to your name (where the Twitterbird used to be). If you select the wrong photo accidentally, don't fret. Just go through the upload process again by repeating Steps 2 and 3, and then clicking Save again.

Select a Theme for Your Profile Page

1. Now it's time to gussy up your page. You're probably not quite ready to design a custom background (such as the one I have on my MarshaCollier Twitter profile page), so Twitter gives you a choice of 20 decorative backgrounds (or *themes*) to use on your page. From the main Settings page, click the Design link.

2. On the resulting Design settings page, you find the 20 different themes that Twitter offers their members to start. Click any of the theme images and your page background changes automatically to the one you selected. **Figure 10-13** shows that I selected a theme with birds (second from the left in the bottom row).

3. Keep selecting themes until you find a background you like — and then click the Save Changes button at the bottom of the page.

 You'll also notice some other options at the bottom of the page to change the background image and design colors. These are advanced settings; it's best to play with them after you've been using Twitter for a while.

If you'd like to get a fancy background for your Twitter page in the future, check out these sites for *free* backgrounds and instructions:

➡ www.custombackgroundsfortwitter.com

➡ www.twitbacks.com

➡ www.twitterbackgrounds.org

➡ www.colourlovers.com/themeleon/twitter

Click a theme to choose it.

Figure 10-13

Set Up Notices

1. On your Twitter Settings page, you see a link for Notices. Click Notices, and you find an area where you can customize how you'd like to be notified when a particular action occurs on your Twitter account.

2. Read the descriptions and click the check box only next to the notices you want to receive. Twitter will send you an e-mail communication when the following things happen:

- **Someone starts following you.** If someone finds you and decides to follow you (I explain how all that happens in Chapter 11), Twitter sends you an e-mail telling you so. If you don't want this e-mail notification, be sure there is no check mark in the box next to New Follower E-mails.

- **You receive a new direct message (DM).** Here's where you decide whether you want your direct messages sent to your cell phone. If you don't want the text messages on your phone (especially if you don't have an unlimited data plan), click to remove the check mark from the box next to Direct Text E-mails.

 Even if you uncheck this box, you still receive DMs to your registered e-mail address. You won't miss a thing. The fun of Twitter, though, is that all the conversation happens in real time. Unless you're checking your e-mail regularly, you won't be in on the immediacy of the experience.

- **Twitter has a newsletter to share.** Occasionally, Twitter's founders and bigwigs like to reach out to users to explain new features on the site, or to let you know about changes in the rules (the Terms of Service, or TOS for short). You really need to know about this stuff, so leave the check in the box next to E-mail Newsletter.

Know Twitter Shorthand

When you decide you'd like to send tweets from your smartphone — or even if you're tweeting on the Web — Twitter has some shorthand commands that can facilitate (shorten) your Twitter messaging experience.

When a direct message (DM) comes to your phone from Twitter, it has a return numeric shortcut of 40404. You can reply to 40404 to tweet, to send a direct message, or perform some other valuable Twitter actions. If you merely send a text message to 40404 without preceding it with one of the commands listed in Table 10-1, your text will simply appear as a Tweet in your Twitter stream.

Table 10-1 shows some shorthand commands you can use to direct an action other than simply posting to your Twitter stream. (I used my Twitter username as an example in the table.)

Table 10-1   Twitter Smartphone Shorthand Commands

Command	How it looks	What it does
FOLLOW *username*	FOLLOW marshacollier	Starts following marshacollier
UNFOLLOW *username*	UNFOLLOW marshacollier	Stops following marshacollier
ON/OFF	ON or OFF	Turns all Tweet notifications on or off
ON/OFF *username*	ON or OFF marshacollier	Turns Tweet notifications for a user on or off
GET *username*	GET marshacollier	Shows the last tweet from user
RT *username*	RT marshacollier	Retweets a user's latest tweet*
FAV *username*	FAV marshacollier	Puts a user's latest tweet on your list of Favorites*
D *username yourmessage*	D marshacollier Hi how are you?	Sends a direct message to a user

* Find more about these functions in Chapter 11.

Conversing on Twitter with Friends, Family, and More

Chapter 11

Get ready to . . .

➠ Follow Basic Guidelines for Conversing.................. 204

➠ Pass Along a Chosen Tweet 206

➠ Favorite Your Favorite Tweets 208

➠ Search for Tweeted Topics........................... 210

➠ Know What to Tweet About 210

When you register on Twitter, you get all sorts of suggestions about how to connect with people. As I suggest in Chapter 10, I think it's best to get familiar with the basic concepts of a new site before inviting all your friends to the party. I mean, after all, what kind of host or hostess can you be if you barely know the lay of the land yourself?

I hope you've checked out Twitter a bit. I must confess, it took me quite a while to really "get" it. But once I did, I wanted to invite all my friends — and if they weren't already on Twitter, I wanted them to join so I could share my new shiny toy!

In this chapter, I talk a little more about the finer details of communicating on Twitter. I give you guidelines about making hip tweets, show you how to retweet and accumulate favorite tweets, and give you some advice on what to tweet about.

Follow Basic Guidelines for Conversing

1. We're all adults here. I'm not going to tell you who to be friends with on Twitter, and I'm certainly not going to tell you what to tweet. There are a few conventions and standards that make Twitter interesting, so read on and you'll be twittering like a pro in no time.

- **Don't just broadcast your ideas.** When you're on Twitter, you'll see that some people just continually broadcast their thoughts over the stream. *Broadcast media is so yesterday!* In 21st-century new media, it's all about conversation and engaging others. Your interaction is with real people — talk to them!

- **Do tweet out ideas and comments.** Since it's all about conversation, give people something to reply to you about. Did you ruin a batch of cookies in the oven? If you're following other people who might be baking cookies, they'll commiserate with you. You have to buy new tires, and you're going through sticker shock? Certainly, in this economy, someone out there can relate.

- **Reply to others.** When someone makes a comment that you're interested in, make a comment back! In **Figure 11-1**, I'm about to reply to the user @Greetums about her soup experience. You can also see my *Latest* (or last) tweet just below the What's Happening text box. I remarked to @Krystyl about how much I liked her new avatar (avatar = picture, remember?).

2. Starting any posting with the at-sign (@), followed by the name of the person you're sending it to, is like putting an address on the tweet: @Krystyl means this tweet is addressed to @Krystyl, as if we were in a conversation. Here's how to reply:

Figure 11-1

1. *When you mouse over the right side of a tweet on your Twitter page, the word* Reply *comes up out of nowhere.* When you click this Reply link (or *swoosh*), the tweeter's ID appears in the What's Happening text box with an at-sign (@) in front of it — for example, @Greetums. These are called @ (at) replies; they're visible to the person you addressed them to, and to the people who follow both of you.

2. *If you want all the people who follow you to see an @ reply, embed it within your tweet. See the example in* **Figure 11-2**, *where I reply to @MakeItWork.*

 Remember that @ replies are not private; the private messages you can send are called *Direct Messages*.

Thank you @MakeitWork for mouse pads (know it sounds stupid, but they're great jar openers 4 kitchen) Maybe a new subsidiary @EricGreenspan?
about 8 hours ago via Seesmic

Figure 11-2

3. *In* **Figure 11-3**, *notice how the message looks after I responded to @Greetums (even though I forgot about the soup).* When you send a tweet like this, the recipient will definitely recognize it as conversation and will most likely respond to you.

MarshaCollier @**Greetums** :) Your matzoh ball tweet just ended up in a screen shot of my upcoming book, Twitter & Facebook For Seniors
less than a minute ago from web

Figure 11-3

3. To see all your @ replies, click the link on the right side of your Twitter home page that has the @ and your ID next to it. **Figure 11-4** shows you what I mean.

Click on your home page for tweets that mention you.

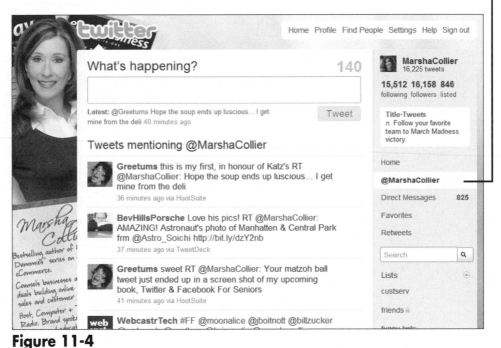

Figure 11-4

Pass Along a Chosen Tweet

1. To make a statement on Twitter is to *tweet*, so to repeat a statement on Twitter is to *RE-tweet*, right? If you see a comment from someone you're following, you can retweet what they said to all your followers. That way, your followers who aren't following the person who made the pithy comment can have the chance to see it, too. (Twitter is all about sharing!)

2. You can retweet (RT) in two ways. You accomplish the classic RT when you copy and paste the original tweet in the What's Happening text box; then type the letters RT before @ and the username of the original tweeter. **Figure 11-5**, shows a couple of interesting comments that I chose to retweet to the people who follow me.

> RT @Annie_Fox Want kids to listen to you? Try listening to them. When you don't model what you teach, you're teaching something else.
> 2 minutes ago via Seesmic
>
> RT @vedo ok, if at first you *do* succeed, try to hide your astonishment.
> 3 minutes ago via Seesmic

Figure 11-5

3. The second (new improved) way to retweet is to find a tweet in your tweet stream (just as you did in the @ reply). Hover your mouse pointer over the right side of the tweet and the word *Retweet* will show up next to a little recycling symbol.

Some people don't like this type of retweeting because they find it harder to tell whether it's a retweet. But it's the only format to use if the original Tweet is too long once you add the RT symbols. **Figure 11-6** shows the difference: Instead of the RT and @ symbol, a recycling icon appears next to my name.

The recycling icon shows up here.

> ☒ **MarshaCollier** AMAZING! Astronaut's photo of Manhatten & Central Park frm @Astro_Soichi http://bit.ly /dzY2nb
> about 2 hours ago via bit.ly
> Retweeted by oronhaus and 1 other

Figure 11-6

If you want to track which of your tweets get retweeted, click the Home link near the top right and go to your home page. On the right, click the Retweets link, and you see a page like the one in **Figure 11-7**. Three tabs on the page classify different tweets. When you click the Your Tweets, Retweeted tab, you can see how many people retweeted your tweet.

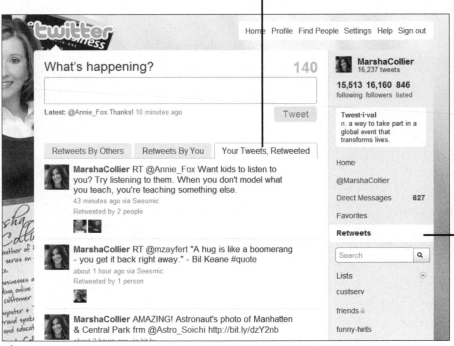

Click here to check out retweets.

Figure 11-7

Favorite Your Favorite Tweets

1. When you see a tweet that strikes your fancy, or a tweet sent to you that makes you smile, Twitter lets you make it a Favorite. You can make any tweet (except a private

Direct Message) a favorite. If you guide your mouse pointer over the tweet, just above where the Reply and Retweet appear on the right, you see a small outline of a star. Click the star, and it turns gold. After you click it, the tweet is saved to your Favorites page.

2. To find the favorites you've *favorited* (that's the Twitter term), click the Home link at the top of the page and go to your home page. The fourth link on the right is Favorites. If you click it, you arrive at the page that lists your favorite tweets. Check out **Figure 11-8**, and you'll see my recent favorites. Notice that all these tweets have a little gold star next to them.

Click to view favorite tweets.

Figure 11-8

Search for Tweeted Topics

1. You can use *hashtags* — words with the pound sign (#) in front of them — in your tweets to simply identify single word topics or abbreviations of events. And you can search to find tweets about the topics or events that are identified this way. For example, if you regularly watch *American Idol* and want to find all tweets about the show, you can search for them by typing **#americanidol** in the search box at the right side of your home page and pressing Enter.

 Because a search is not case-sensitive, you could also type #AmericanIdol or #AMERICANIDOL and get the same results. What you won't get in your search results are tweets such as "*American* President Obama is the *idol* of millions" because the words aren't together and preceded by the hashtag.

2. You can append your tweets with hashtags to join in Twitter chats that take place on a planned, regular basis. I participate in a weekly Twitter chat about customer service. (Yes, I tell you all about how to participate in chats in Chapter 12.) Because participants have only 140 characters per tweet, we shorten *customer service* to *#custserv* so the hashtag takes up less space. (Hastags get a message across in a much more concise manner.) In **Figure 11-9**, I typed **#custserv** into the search box on the right side of my home page and all tweets with #custserv showed up.

Know What to Tweet About

I know that when you're new on Twitter (you're called a *newbie*), you want to join in the fun but maybe you can't think of anything to tweet about. It's a frustrating feeling — know that I feel your pain. Even now, I often face the blank What's Happening text box with nothing in my head.

Type a topic here to search for tweets.

Figure 11-9

Check out this bullet list for some good ideas about common ways to start a Twitter conversation:

➡ **Share quotes**. People on Twitter just love to read quotes by famous people. The quotes can be funny or inspirational. If you can't think of any off the top of your head, just search Google for the word *quote* and the name of your favorite smart person. For example search *quote Joan Rivers* or *quote Eleanor Roosevelt*. (Searching for quotes from either of these women will no doubt net you some doozies!) When you tweet a good quote, people will no doubt retweet it to their followers. When more people see how pithy you are, they may follow you, too. I retweeted a quote that I saw on Twitter today (see **Figure 11-10**).

LoriMoreno There is only one happiness in life, to love and be loved. ~George Sand #quote
10 minutes ago via SocialOomph

Figure 11-10

➡ **Ask questions**. If you are curious about something or just want to know what other people think about a subject, ask a question. In **Figure 11-11**, my friend @Lotay asked a question about the iPad. Notice, he used the word Poll and a hashtag preceding it. You don't have to use either. People will know what a question is! By the way, he got 18 responses.

lotay #Poll: Will you buy an Apple iPad?
30 minutes ago from UberTwitter

Figure 11-11

➡ **Share music.** Remember how much fun it used to be when you'd sit on the floor with your friends and play records? I love listening to Nina Simone, and in **Figure 11-12**, my friend Melissa tweeted out one of her songs. You can do that on Twitter (I do this often) by tweeting links to recorded music. When someone clicks the link in your tweet, he or she lands on a Web site that plays the music! In Chapter 13, I show you how to find and link to music.

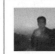

MelissaRowley listening to "Nina Simone - Feeling Good" ♫ http://blip.fm/~o2lto
31 minutes ago via Blip.fm

Figure 11-12

➠ **Share a funny "overheard."** What's an *overheard?*
Have you ever been in the supermarket and overheard someone say something that makes you want
to laugh out loud? That something is an overheard.
When you post an overheard on Twitter, you abbreviate the words to just OH. In **Figure 11-13**, I think
@Ed must have been listening to his buddies at the
barbershop!

Ed OH: "We MADE the generation that made the Google
and Facebook and Twitter and iPads. I think we can
handle them!"
half a minute ago via web

Figure 11-13

➠ **Pass on a news story.** There are so many great arti-
cles on the Internet, and news stories come to mind
almost immediately. Why not send out an interesting article to your friends? I love cooking, so when I
saw the tweet in **Figure 11-14**, I clicked the link to
see the story on Julia Child.

foodphilosophy Here's why I love her, FYI. Julia Child:
Boutez en Avant http://bit.ly/dp5Z47
23 minutes ago via Tweetie

Figure 11-14

You will notice that the link looks a little like gib-
berish. That's because the Web address for the
story was shortened. In Chapter 13, I show you
how to shorten long URLs for your tweets.

➠ **Show off your pictures.** Everyone on Twitter loves
to share photos. In **Figure 11-15**, I tweeted a link to
a picture of some lovely flowers in my garden on

Easter. People on Twitter know that the link contains pictures because it points to the Twitpic Web site where people upload their photos. I tell you about Twitpic in Chapter 13.

 MarshaCollier **Happy Easter** from my **garden**. http://twitpic.com/1d0ut8

about 5 hours ago from Seesmic

Figure 11-15

Gathering Tools of the Twitter Trade

Chapter 12

Now that you're on Twitter and you're building a small group of friends, you'll see that you want to do even more. I'll bet you'd enjoy following even more people, right?

Some people feel that if they have a small group of friends, they can manage conversing easily — but sometimes it's okay to branch out and meet more. In this chapter, I show you how to make groups (lists) of different people so you can focus certain Twitter conversations on certain friends. And, I introduce a couple of applications that you can install on your computer and use to see everything that's going on — no matter how many people you follow.

Let's really call this chapter *Twitter — the Advanced Course*. But don't let that scare you. I show you some simple ways to enhance your tweeting experience. And you needn't spend any money on extra tools; I explain how to do just about anything you can on Twitter.

Get ready to. . .

➠ Search for Tweeps on WeFollow 216

➠ Add Yourself to WeFollow 221

➠ Find Trends with Summize 222

➠ FollowFriday, FF, and Other Hashtags 226

➠ Connect with People 230

➠ Keep Track of Hundreds, Thousands of Friends? 232

➠ View Your Friend Lists........ 235

Search for Tweeps on WeFollow

1. I'm a big believer in "the more, the merrier." Although I don't always see everything that everyone on Twitter says,

> I always have the option to listen and reply to those who are not on my list of closest friends. So, if you're looking for that option, check out *WeFollow*, a user-powered directory of Twitter peeps (known as *Tweeps*). Not *everyone* is listed — only over 800,000 people.

> Considering that Twitter has over 8 million users, I feel this site gives me an idea of the more active and interesting ones. You can find not only celebrities, but also people who have common interests and share the kind of hobbies you like.

2. Type **www.wefollow.com** into your Web browser. When the page loads, you have a decision to make. **Figure 12-1** shows you the window you see. You can visit the site just to browse, or you can add yourself to the directory so that others will find you. I suggest that you just browse to start by clicking the Not Now, Just Browsing button. (Baby steps, right?)

3. When you land on the opening page shown in **Figure 12-2**, you'll see a lot of information. Several of the more popular categories (of the thousands listed on the site) appear here — along with the people, in order of influence, who've been listed in each category (or *tag,* as it's also called).

> Some Twitter directories list users by number of followers. Okay, any monkey — with enough effort and time — can accumulate a following of thousands of people. The deal on Twitter is to find *influential* people. Influential Twitter users are ranked according to the interesting things they say (other people retweet their tweets), their interaction with others via @ conversations, and the fair amount of time they spend on the site to engage new people.

Click here to start out just browsing.

Figure 12-1

4. On the right of the opening page are two boxes you can use to find people you want to follow:

- **Top Tags:** The most popular tags (or categories) that people search through for people to follow on the site. To see more? Click the More Tags link at the bottom of the box.

- **Top Cities:** If you'd like to make more friends in your local area, use this list to see cities in order of their popularity on the site. If you don't see your city, click the More Cities link.

     When you click a city (I clicked New York, NY in **Figure 12-3**), you see a list of New York City Twitter users shown in the order of their influence on the site.

Check out the users in a category.   Type a keyword here to find a category.

Figure 12-2

5. At the top of the page, you find a gray box that says *Enter a tag*. Here you can type in any subject you wish. As you type, a drop-down list appears and shows you categories that match what you're typing — and how many people are in the category. Click a category from this list to view its influential users.

I started typing eBay and discovered that the single tag *eBay* (rather than *ebayseller*, *ebaypowerseller*, and so on) showed the most people in the tags mentioning eBay. I clicked the eBay category — and was sent to a page of users (**Figure 12-4**), listed in order of influence, who have categorized themselves with the eBay tag. To find out more about any of these people, click a name.

wefollow   🔍 Enter a tag...

New York, NY   4,370 Users

| Most Influential | Most Followers |

#1 **themoment**   1,590,832 followers
    Where Style Meets Culture

#2 **cutblog**   52,619 followers
    New York magazine's fashion blog   + 405 NEW

#3 **Newsweek**   1,226,606 followers
    Newsweek magazine's daily news, blogs, photo   + 163 NEW
    galleries, audio and vide...

#4 **THEREALSWIZZZ**   159,487 followers
    THE BEST   + 277 NEW

#5 **someecards**   1,607,731 followers
    Welcome to the Twitter feed of somewhat acclaimed
    humor site, someecards...

#6 **grubstreetny**   7,609 followers
    New York magazine's food and restaurant blog   + 25 NEW

#7 **RollingStone**   90,938 followers
    The official Twitter of Rolling Stone magazine and   + 196 NEW
    RollingStone.com.

#8 EverythingNYC **EverythingNYC**
                   I ♥ NYC. The Greatest City in the World.
    6,504 followers

Figure 12-3

6. Clicking a user in the category's list (in the eBay category, I clicked my name — MarshaCollier) will bring you to a page (**Figure 12-5**) that shows the user's one-line Twitter bio, avatar, basic information, and a list of the categories they're tagged in. If, after looking at the info, you want to follow the user, click the green *Follow this user* bar under the avatar (photo).

7. Rinse and repeat. Ooops, I mean *perform these searches over and over*, and you can find lots of interesting new people to follow.

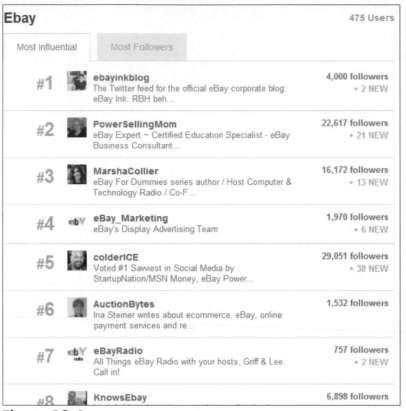

Figure 12-4

8. You like shortcuts? Me too. If you want to get a little daring, make a list of categories you're interested in and search directly from your browser. In the browser's address bar, type the **wefollow.com** address, followed by a forward slash (/) and then a category tag from your list. The result will look like this URL (except it'll show your category; here I wanted to find people interested in gardening):

```
http://wefollow.com/twitter/gardening
```

 If there's no category tagged with your subject, try another. This maneuver works most of the time. But keep in mind that tags are only one word — so if you want to search for people who are into *interior design*, you'll use the tag *interiordesign*.

Click here to follow a WeFollow user.

Marsha Collier

eBay For Dummies series author / Host Computer & Technology Radio / Co-Founder #CustServ Chat / Customer Service & Social Media Influencer / Fitness Nut

Basic Information

| Followers | 16,172 | Following | 15,525 | Updates | 16,305 |

Interests Rankings

tech
Ranking: #854 of 24,818

Recent followers (15 total)

ecommerce
Ranking: #21 of 1,518

Recent followers (16 total)

ebay
Ranking: #3 of 500

Recent followers (30 total)

Figure 12-5

Add Yourself to WeFollow

1. Here's how to add yourself on WeFollow for other new users to find. Type **www.twitter.com** in your browser's address bar and press Enter. Then log in to Twitter. Open another browser tab, type **www.wefollow.com** in that tab's address bar, and press Enter.

2. At WeFollow, click the green Add Yourself to WeFollow button that appears at the top of every page.

3. Allow WeFollow to access your Twitter account by clicking the Allow button, as in **Figure 12-6**. This is safe to do; you aren't revealing your password to a new site.

4. On the next page, WeFollow asks you to input your home city and up to five different tags of subjects you're interested in.

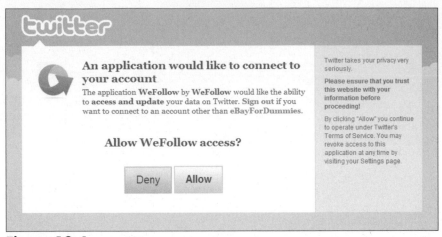

Figure 12-6

5. Click Send (when you're done) and WeFollow sends a tweet to your tweetstream, announcing to the world you are listed on WeFollow.

Find Trends with Summize

1. Summize is Twitter's own outside search capability. You can do search after search directly from your Twitter home page, but Summize does a much better job searching by keywords and trends. Type **www.summize.com** into your Web browser and press Enter; you're transported to search.twitter.com.

2. The resulting page is pretty blank, so I won't bore you with a screen shot. Just type a subject that intrigues you into the text box and click Search. I typed in *cookies* (as in chocolate-chip and oatmeal-raisin); I'm in the mood to see who else is baking some cookies.

3. You arrive at the search results page and see all the current tweets that have the word *cookies* in them, as in **Figure 12-7**. You can click any ID you see there to be transported to that person's Twitter page and take a look at his or her stream.

See your topic in tweets here.   Type a topic here.

Figure 12-7

4. Then, if this new person's tweets interest you, go ahead and follow the person on Twitter (it's not just okay, it's the expected thing).

5. Notice on the right side of the page you see the following sections:

- **Show tweets written in (select language):** From the drop-down menu, you may select from a list of 19 different languages to search. The default is English, but if you'd like to meet people who tweet in French, select French.

- **Translate:** If you've selected to view foreign language tweets, (I searched for tweets posted in Spanish) and you're not too clear about the translation, Click this link and it translates all the tweets on the page to English. Translations are highlighted, as in **Figure 12-8**.

- **Trending Topics:** These are the topics currently most tweeted (or bandied) about on the site. As I was writing this chapter, I felt a large earthquake that was centered in Mexico, followed by nine aftershock quakes. *Earthquake* became a trending topic on Twitter — and through Twitter search, I found the tweets about *earthquakes* shown in **Figure 12-9**.

Translate to English.

Choose a language.

Figure 12-8

Real-time results for **earthquake**   ⊕ Save this search

erinyoungren Aaaaand an aftershock... ? #**earthquake**
less than 20 seconds ago from TweetDeck

hestaprynnmusic 6.9 **earthquake**?? Please don't tell me
Vince Vaughn is going to sing again.
less than 20 seconds ago from web

Metblogs [all city] Los Angeles Metblogs : 6.9 **Earthquake**
in Baja California http://bit.ly/dc8YNQ
less than 20 seconds ago from twitterfeed

Pinkgineer 3.6 **Earthquake** in Julian, CA
less than 20 seconds ago from Brizzly

jodenaire another **earthquake** #sheessh!
less than 20 seconds ago from web

ZAmmi More #**earthquake** damage #bajaquake
http://tweetphoto.com/17193148 (Via @elviiira)
less than 20 seconds ago from txt

ScanMyPhotos If you felt the #**Earthquake**, clickon this
link and register your location for USGA tracking:
http://ow.ly/1uwK9
less than 20 seconds ago from HootSuite

nateritter Stop the world...I wanna get off. #sandiego
#**earthquake** (via @SDTechGirl)
less than 20 seconds ago from Tweetie

Figure 12-9

- **Nifty Queries:** A list of interesting queries recently
  performed in Twitter search. Check 'em out for a little
  amusement.

Notice that when the search results page lists a tweet
as an @ reply to another person, both people's avatars (pictures) appear on the left side of the tweet.

FollowFriday, FF, and Other Hashtags

1. When you've been on Twitter long enough, you'll see tweets from people with hashtags (#) preceding them. The hashtag may be followed by strange abbreviations, severalwordsthatruntogether (say what?), or single topics. Hashtags help to spread and organize information on Twitter.

    Using hashtags makes subjects easier to search for and find. Conferences, major events, and even disasters (such as #swineflu) use hashtags to put specific tweets in order and make it easier for you — and your followers — to follow.

2. Here's a list of some Twitter hash tags and what they refer to. After you look at the list, you'll get the drift. You can find more, along with their activity and the top members at What the Hashtag? (`http://wthashtag.com`) a user-editable encyclopedia for hashtags found on Twitter. After that, I give you some conventions to follow when creating your own hashtags.

   • **#sxsw** — A popular conference, South By Southwest, is too long to tweet since tweets are limited to 140 characters. People at the conference include `#sxsw` in their tweets to show where they are and what they're doing there.

   • **#CES** — Consumer Electronics Show. Again, too long to tweet. Let your friends know you're talking about it by using #CES

   • **#musicmonday** — On Mondays, Twitter users like to tweet their favorite songs. It's like sitting around a record player (remember?) with your friends. Tweets have a link to a playable version of the song.

- **#FF or #FollowFriday** — Do you have someone you really like to follow? Someone who often puts up interesting tweets? Recommend that person to your followers by tweeting his or her ID, followed by the hash tag.

 Remember: Only do this on Fridays. Consider the people in your Twitter stream who may not approve your own private daily version of #FollowFriday.

- **#earthquake** — When someone feels the ground shake, they usually just tweet @EARTHQUAKE because they're too freaked to say anything else. People follow up with information on damage, provide brief news reports, and append their tweets with this hash tag.

- **#tcot** — *Top Conservatives on Twitter*. This hash tag is used by a very vocal and interesting group. If you tweet something with a politically conservative slant, add this hashtag to your tweet. You're bound to get more like minded followers.

- **#p2** — The #p2 hashtag stands for *Progressives 2.0*. Their official mission statement says "a resource for progressives using social media who prioritize diversity and empowerment, the 'progressive batchannel,' and an umbrella tag for information for progressives on Twitter."

- **#tlot** — *Top Libertarians on Twitter*. What more can I say?

- **#custserv** — A hashtag for the Customer Service chat. People participate in chats on Twitter at prescribed times each week. When they take part in the chat, they follow each tweet with the #custserv tag.

Rather than using search during chats, people use sites like Twubs (`http://twubs.com`), What the Hashtag? (`http://wthashtag.com`), or TweetChat (`http://tweetchat.com`) where they can see the tweets and respond to them in real time. These sites also insert the hashtag at the end of your tweets automatically. **Figure 12-10** shows the Twubs page for our #custserv chat.

3. There are many weekly chats on Twitter, and you might find one you'd like to take part in. You may use Twitter search to find a chat you might want to join. **Figure 12-11** shows a search for #petchat. Here are a few examples of chats:

Figure 12-10

- **#gardenchat** — all things gardening.

- **#dogtalk** — pictures of dogs, dog tips, and dog news.

- **#petchat** — for the rest of the animal world.

- **#blogchat** — Stating a blog? Run by blog expert @MackCollier, this chat is full of tips and ideas.

- **#journchat** — People in public relations, journalism, and related fields meet to talk.

- **#carchat** — love your car? There's a group for you too!

- **#americanidol** — Watching *American Idol* on TV by yourself? Want to make a comment and possibly get an answer? Incorporate the TV show name with a hash mark in front and look for others.

Figure 12-11

- **#sexonaplate** — Hash tag used by @FoodPhilosophy (Jennifer Iannolo, CEO of the Culinary Media Network) when she tweets about an exotic plate of food.

- **#jobs** — Looking for a job? Search for tweets with this hash tag.

- **#quote** — When you post a quote as a tweet, follow it with the #quote hash tag for quote-lovers to find.

 Keep in mind that hashtags should be used sporadically (unless you are in the middle of a live chat). They're kind of annoying to look at, and lose meaning when used superfluously.

Connect with People

Did someone @ reply to you, and you decide you want to know more about that person? See a tweet you like? Want to know if you're following someone? Want to see who's following you? Twitter has a quick and easy tool you can use to find out more.

1. On your Twitter home page, click the link on the right side that has the @ sign followed by your Twitter ID. You'll see a list of people who have mentioned you in their tweets.

2. If you want to know more about someone (whether that person is following you, or you're doing the following, or who's following whom), put your mouse over his or her ID or avatar. An information box like the one in **Figure 12-12** appears. If you're not following the person, you see a gray Follow button; if you are following, you see a check mark and the words *You Follow*.

Find out whether you follow this user.

Tweets mentioning @MarshaCollier

MegOyanagi TK! @calbosch: #FF BEAUTIFUL WOMEN
@MomsofAmerica @IKching @KathyNelson
@littlebytesnews @libbytalks @MegOyanagi @cathzz
@MarshaCollier...
3 minutes ago via HootSuite

MomsofAmerica   llier Your welcome! #FF
debra cincioni   to MarshaCollier
USA more...

✓ You follow ⊡ ⊠   ⚙▾   FRIENDS @mindler1
                                              erica @billsellars
@FIZZyDuck
9 minutes ago via web

haydenblack @MarshaCollier you really should get out
more.
15 minutes ago via web in reply to MarshaCollier

calbosch #FF BEAUTIFUL WOMEN @MomsofAmerica
@IKching @KathyNelson @littlebytesnews @libbytalks
@MegOyanagi @cathzz @MarshaCollier
@ELMLs_Angels
17 minutes ago via web

lacorbeau RT @MarshaCollier It's going to be another
"writing until 2 am" night *sigh* (sorry if I don't tweet
much) <know what that's like :)>
17 minutes ago via web

Figure 12-12

3. Before you follow someone you don't know, click the
More link next to his or her location; the person's full
Twitter information shows up in a small box (shown in
Figure 12-13). If you like what you see, go ahead and
follow.

4. If you do follow this new person — and want to know if
he or she is following you — just click the little cogwheel
(indicating settings). A menu like the one in **Figure 12-14**
drops down, showing the next steps to take.

If the menu says that you *can* Direct Message this person,
then your answer is yes: Anyone you can send a Direct
Message *is* following you.

Figure 12-13

Figure 12-14

Keep Track of Hundreds, Thousands of Friends?

It's a challenge, but you'll soon be following more people than you could possibly imagine at the moment (unless you're channeling Cecil B. DeMille). The more the merrier? Sometimes. You may want to monitor a smaller group of real-life or business friends, and if you follow hundreds of people, you may never see their tweets.

1. Enter (behold!) *Twitter Lists.* You're allowed to make lists of as many people as you wish. You can choose to make them public or private. If they're private, no one can find out that they're not on the list of your personal friends (which can be tactful). Start your lists by going to your Twitter home page. Scroll down the page. Below the Search box, you'll see the Lists heading.

2. Click the New List link. A window appears, as shown in **Figure 12-15**. In the boxes provided, give your list a name and a short description. Typing a description for a private list isn't necessary (because you know what the list is about); doing so is optional in that case.

After you type in a name, the List link appears below the Title box.

Select a privacy setting.

Name your list.

Figure 12-15

3. Select the Private option and only you can access the list (by clicking the link that appears under the Lists heading on the right side of your home page). If you want to share your list with others — the way I do with my Funny-twits list — click the Public option. That way other folks can follow the people on your list.

4. After you make a list, you'll want to add people to it. Here's the procedure:

1. *You can either search for people in the Find People area (well, yeah) at the top of the page, or click a new person's ID when he or she comes up in the Twitter stream.* Clicking the ID brings you to the new person's Profile page, where you'll see a bio and other such information.

2. *At the top of the Profile page, under the person's name, is a Lists drop-down list.* Click it and any lists you've made show up here.

3. *Select the list to which you want to add this person — and click the small box next to it.* Notice (in **Figure 12-16**) a tiny lock icon next to my Friends list; it means I can see the list but no one else can.

Choose a list here.

Figure 12-16

You'll also see that you can make a new list for the person you're adding; that option is available in the drop-down menu. This is very handy if you haven't set up a list yet.

4. *After you click the box, the menu will close.* Under the newly added person's name, you'll see his or her page — which shows (only to you) that this person is on one of your lists. **Figure 12-17** shows what that looks like.

Figure 12-17

View Your Friend Lists

1. Now that you've made your sooper-secret list of those you follow, you want to be able to watch your friends' tweets, right? That's the easy part. You start on your Twitter home page, under the Lists heading, with the lists you've made. Clicking the name of a list shows you tweets from just the friends you've selected to be on the list.

2. Pretty cool, eh? But (there's always a *but*) you can't see the tweets from the other people you follow — *or* your Direct Messages *or* your @ replies! What to do? You're going to have to download some Twitter client software. But don't worry, those programs are *free* and safe to

install on your computer. This software allows you to see all your Tweets, all at once.

3. There are many different programs, but two are the most popular: Seesmic and TweetDeck. They operate very much in the same way, but you have to decide which you prefer. One may be easier to read, or you may like the way the user IDs look on the other. Here are a couple of features to note about these programs:

- Twitter client programs update tweets automatically and allow you to have separate columns for @ replies, Direct Messages (private messages), your lists, your Followers, and your searches. You're limited only by the amount of space on your desktop (and how good your eyes are). They do allow you to scroll back and forth to view all the columns.

- The software also makes a noise: a bird tweet in TweetDeck and a chime in Seesmic. You'll hear it automatically when you get an @ reply or a Direct Message. You can turn it off, of course, but that way… you'll never know when someone is trying to reach you.

- You can send tweets while you're using these programs, and do anything you can do on Twitter — the only difference is that you can see everything you're doing all at once. Call it a bird's-eye view.

4. **Figure 12-18** shows you Seesmic on my desktop. Notice that I have columns for my @ Replies, my @MarshaCollier/Friends private list and my Home, which consists of everyone I follow. (You didn't really think I'd let you see my private Direct Messages, did you?)

Figure 12-18

The other client, TweetDeck (**Figure 12-19**), handles
everything the same way. The major differences are that
you can change the colors of the TweetDeck screen, it
auto shortens your links, allows you to post to Facebook
(and other social media platforms), and has the controls
and settings in the upper-right corner of the screen, ver
sus the lower-left corner in Seesmic.

5. You can download TweetDeck at www.tweetdeck.com
and Seesmic at seesmic.com. Check them both out and
see what works best for you.

Figure 12-19

Part IV
The Rest of the Social Networking Story

The 5th Wave   By Rich Tennant

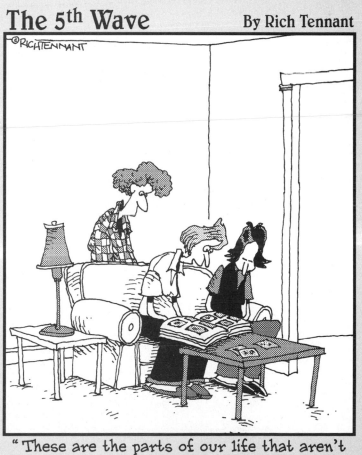

"These are the parts of our life that aren't on YouTube."

Sharing (and Grabbing) Photos, Videos, and Music

Chapter 13

Get ready to ...

➡ Give Credit When You Share 242

➡ Make Your Links Short 245

➡ Share Your Photos with Twitpic 250

➡ Become an Online Deejay (DJ) 254

➡ Spin Your Songs for Online Friends 256

➡ Find and Share Videos on YouTube 258

One of the most fun ways to share online, in both Twitter and Facebook, is to share your favorite music and images. We've talked about sharing your own photos on Facebook, but how about treating your online friends to some of the unique items you run across elsewhere on the Web? You could share a news story, a song, or a funny video — pretty much any cool thing you find!

I've spent many evenings online with friends, pointing from a song to a video to a story. It's the 21st century version of a coffee klatch; it's also like sharing a bottle of wine with friends (only you get to drink the entire bottle if you wish).

In this chapter, I give you some advice for mannerly and efficient sharing, go over some great places to find material to share, and tell you how to easily transport the treasures you find to your Facebook or Twitter page.

Give Credit When You Share

1. I want to talk a little about the conventions — or, better yet, the etiquette — for sharing what you find online. Odds are if you hijack someone's article or photo from somewhere on the Internet, that person may never know it — but *you* will. Good manners (believe it or not) are still in fashion, but they follow new rules. Please credit any Web site and the person behind the post when you share the content. You can generally do so by including a link back to the original posting of the content, or in the case of Twitter, thank the person who originally posted it.

 I posted a video that Chris Brogan originally posted on his blog to a couple of places: my Facebook page and my own blog. Plus, I tweeted about it on Twitter. **Figure 13-1** shows how I handled giving credit on my Facebook page.

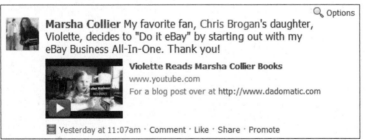

Marsha Collier My favorite fan, Chris Brogan's daughter, Violette, decides to "Do it eBay" by starting out with my eBay Business All-In-One. Thank you!

Violette Reads Marsha Collier Books
www.youtube.com
For a blog post over at http://www.dadomatic.com

Yesterday at 11:07am · Comment · Like · Share · Promote

Figure 13-1

2. When you want to link to a YouTube video (see the later task "Find and Share Videos on YouTube" for more information), you can type the @ (at sign) before you type the name you want to credit. When you do that on Facebook, the names of your friends show up in a drop-down menu. **Figure 13-2** shows how that works. When you see the person's name you want to include, click it, and the full name appears in your post. Doing this also causes the post to appear on your friend's Profile page. It's what the kids call *giving a little Facebook love*.

Start typing the name here.   Choose from your list of friends.

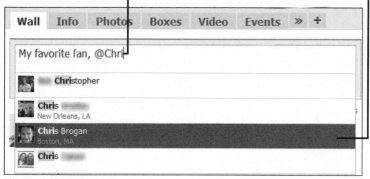

Figure 13-2

3. Suppose you want to share a video elsewhere online, as I did a few days later when I posted Chris's video on my blog (yes, I *really* liked it). Besides mentioning the original poster by name in your blog text (see **Figure 13-3**), you can include the name in the keywords area of your blog. (Chapter 15 tells you all about blogs.) And when you do, the credit gets back to him or her through Google mentions.

Credit your source in your posts.

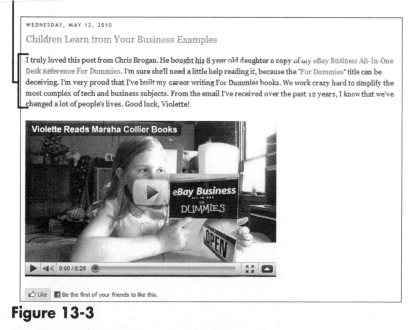

Figure 13-3

4. When you're looking around on the Web, you'll no doubt see a Creative Commons license badge on independent Web sites. *Creative Commons* is a nonprofit organization that works to increase the amount of content *"in the commons* — the body of work that is available to the public for free and legal sharing, use, repurposing, and remixing."* When you see a Creative Commons license icon, click it, and you'll be brought to a page where the actual license appears. This license tells you if there are any restrictions about the content that you may want to share.

Figure 13-4 shows the license that appears on my Facebook page. I really love to share, but I want to make it clear that images of mine cannot be used commercially by anyone.

Figure 13-4

The creative Commons license is represented by three basic icons, and the license details are based on the order in which the icons appear. Table 13-1 outlines a simple shortcut to the Creative Commons license rules.

Table 13-1	**Creative Commons License Icons**	
License Icons	*Stand For ...*	*Which Means ...*
🛈	Attribution	You may distribute, remix, tweak, and build upon the work, even commercially, as long as you credit the original creation.
🛈 ↻	Attribution — Share Alike	All of the above, with this caveat: You credit and license new creations under the identical terms.

License Icons	Stand For ...	Which Means ...
	Attribution — No Derivatives	You may redistribute, commercial and non-commercial, as long as the work is passed along unchanged and in whole, with credit to author.
	Attribution — Non-Commercial	You may remix, tweak, and build upon the work non-commercially only.
	Attribution — Non-Commercial — Share Alike	You may remix, tweak, and build upon the work non-commercially, as long as you credit and license new creations under the identical terms. You can download and redistribute the work as is, but you can also translate, make remixes, and produce new creations based on the work.
	Attribution — Non-Commercial — No Derivatives	This license is often called the *free advertising license* because it allows download of works and sharing as long as the distributor credits and links back to the original. The work can't be changed in any way or used commercially.

Make Your Links Short

Since we're talking Twitter here and you have only 140 characters for every tweet, using up your characters with a long Web address (and you know they can be long) is just wasteful. Even in e-mail messages and Web postings elsewhere, typing in a gigantic URL can be a real chore.

There's an app for that! Several online services will abbreviate any Web address to a nice, manageable size. You may have seen some shortened URLs when you were perusing Twitter. See any Web links that look nonsensical, with no legible words? Clicking that silly-looking link will get you where you want to go, via the magic technology of the webby-tubes.

 Two major URL shorteners — tinyurl.com and bit.ly — are in use currently. I use bit.ly because it's integrated into every Twitter application I use on my computer and mobile phone. Also, bit.ly gives you an information page where you can see how many people click your link after you publish it. (If you use TweetDeck for posting, it will automatically shorten your links with bit.ly).

For example, the Web address for my radio show is

```
http://www.wsradio.com/internet-talk-
   radio.cfm/shows/Computer-and-
   Technology-Radio.html
```

If I use the URL-shortening application from the bit.ly Web site, it looks like this

```
http://bit.ly/3ClAu
```

If I'm Twittering about my radio show, at least the link from bit.ly gives me room to mention the guests.

1. Want to give bit.ly a try? Find a nice long URL that you'd like to shorten, type **http://bit.ly** into your Web browser, and press Enter. You'll arrive at the bit.ly site, as shown in **Figure 13-5**.

 I recommend registering with bit.ly; I promise it's safe, and the site has never sent me any spam. This way, if you want to use your shortened URL in Twitter, you'll be able to send the Tweet directly from the bit.ly page.

2. Start the bit.ly registration process by clicking the Create a Free Account link in the center of the screen. On the resulting page, type in a username, e-mail address, and password

as prompted. You can also automatically create an account using your existing Twitter or Facebook accounts.

Click here to register.

Figure 13-5

3. When you're done filling in the usual items, click Sign Up, and you're in — that's all there is to it! You're automatically transported back to the bit.ly home page, but now it will look a little different.

4. Now copy the URL you want to shorten from its Web page: Click to highlight it, and then press the Ctrl and C keys together. Switch over to the bit.ly site and place your cursor in the text box that says *Paste a Link Here*. Paste your long URL in the box by pressing the Ctrl and V keys together.

5. Your long URL turns into a magically shortened one. If you plan to use the shortened URL in an e-mail, merely click the button marked with the e-mail icon, and the new URL is automatically placed into your e-mail message.

6. If you'd like to tweet the friendlier URL, click the Twitter bird button. You can type the rest of your tweet in the text box (as in **Figure 13-6**) and bit.ly automatically generates a tweet with the link embedded. Use bit.ly each time you come across an interesting news story, article, or video on the Web. It'll save you a lot of typing and it'll make sharing much easier.

 A numeric countdown in the upper-left corner of the text box shows a number that decreases with each character you type. This number shows you how many more characters you have left before you max out your 140-character tweet.

7. Click the Tweet button, and your tweet will autopost instantaneously to your Twitter-stream. **Figure 13-7** shows you the properly tweeted tweet.

8. When you go back to your bit.ly page a little later, you can see how many people clicked your link to check it out. I checked the page an hour later and saw the info in **Figure 13-8**. If you click the Info Page link next to anything you've tweeted from bit.ly, you get an hour-by-hour report on the action. Kinda interesting.

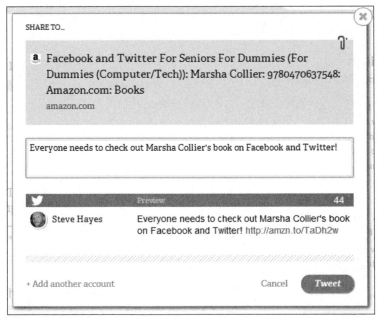

Figure 13-6

Quick etiquette tip? How to Treat Your Waitress http://bit.ly
/b4Q3ob

about 1 hour ago via bit.ly

Figure 13-7

Link History: 1 - 10 of 501

▄▄▄▄▄▄██ 388 clicks this week

Clicks	Links		Info Plus	Date	Options
16 out of 22	How to Treat Your Waitress - Start by looking her in the eye MarshaCollier: Quick etiquette tip? How to Treat Your Waitress http://bit.ly/b4Q3ob		Info Page+	6 hours ago	Options ⚙
35 out of 35	Thank you #140conf and Yahoo! - Marsha Collier		Info Page+	1 day ago	Options ⚙
38 out of 38	Pipes: Marsha Collier's SMurB (Social Media ur Brand)		Info Page+	1 day ago	Options ⚙

Figure 13-8

Also, using bit.ly is a great way to shorten your own Web link in your Twitter profile. (If you don't have a blog or Web site, you can set up a free Google profile as I did at www.google.com/profiles; more on that in Chapter 15.) After you've put a bit.ly link in your profile, you can go back to bit.ly and view the statistics that show how many people visited your page. **Figure 13-9** shows my stats for a week.

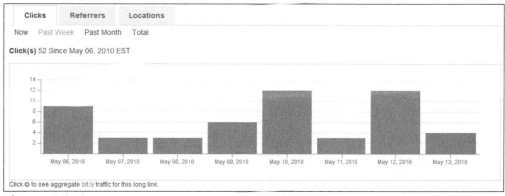

Figure 13-9

Share Your Photos with Twitpic

1. You can find many online sites for sharing your personal photos, but the most popular (especially for mobile phone uploads) is Twitpic. I use Twitpic from my phone and computer, but generally use it for spur-of-the-moment photos only. Photographs that I want as a permanent part of my Facebook page I upload directly to Facebook. You can send mobile uploads to all services, but Twitpic is handy because it's integrated into Twitter — and it gives the image a shortened URL that you can use anywhere.

 I encourage you to join Twitpic before you have a photo to post; doing so will make your first upload move quicker.

2. Joining is so easy. Type **www.twitpic.com** into your Web browser's address box, press Enter, and you see a page similar to the one shown in **Figure 13-10.**

Click here to create an account.

Figure 13-10

3. On the Twitpic home page, click the Create an Account or Login button near the top right. Assuming you're a member of Twitter and you're not currently signed in, a screen like **Figure 13-11** appears.

Click Sign In. Type you Twitter ID and password here.

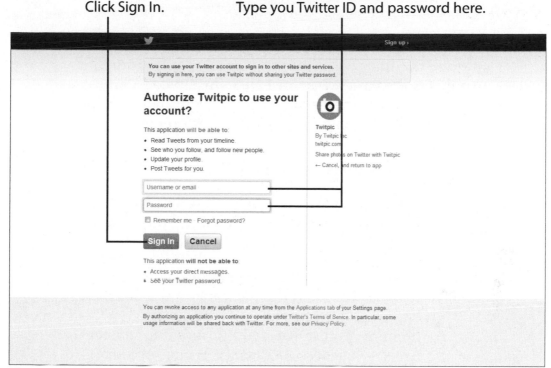

Figure 13-11

4. Type your Twitter ID and password into the appropriate boxes, and click Sign In. Doing so gives Twitpic permission to integrate with your Twitter account. You return to your Twitpic home page automatically, and you're ready to roll.

You'll often be asked to sign in to a site with your Twitter account, as on the bit.ly page (see the preceding section). This safe practice uses the *OAuth protocol*, which enables users to approve that the application may act on their behalf without sharing their password. You can find more information about OAuth at `http://oauth.net`.

5. You can now send a picture in two ways:

a. *Upload from your computer.* If you're at your computer and the image you want to post is on your computer, this is the easiest way. Just click the Upload Photo or Video link at the top right of the page. Then click the Select Media button to find the image on your computer. After you select the picture you want to post online, type a message to accompany it in the Add a Message and Post It text box (what you type appears on the page with your photo). See **Figure 13-12** for an idea of what that looks like. Click the Upload button, and the photo will transport to Twitpic.

 Before you click the Upload button, decide whether you want the picture to immediately appear as a tweet with your text. If you don't — perhaps because you want to save it for a later tweet — uncheck the Post to Twitter Account check box before you click Upload.

Type your message here.　　Click here to find a photo or video.

Upload Photo or Video　　　　　　　　　　×

Select photo or video

Select Media

Ready to upload ChloCenterpiece.jpg (117KB) as an image
We take GIF, JPG, & PNG images up to 10MB in size, and videos up to 3:00 in length in most formats.
Having problems uploading? Try the simple uploader instead.

Caption　　　　　　　　　　　　　　　　90 (twitter limit only)

My cat loves to explore.

Post Options

☐ Set Location (if available)

Share to

☑ Twitter　　Connect with Facebook

Upload

Figure 13-12

The picture posts with your comment and shortened link to the photo's page of your Twitter account. **Figure 13-13** shows you what it looks like. *Note:* The tweet is sent *via Twitpic*.

Two palm trees that have Jasmine trained to cover their trunks, a 15 year project. :) http://twitpic.com/1nc16u
5 minutes ago via Twitpic

Figure 13-13

b. *E-mail the image.* If you'd like to send a picture that you've just taken directly from your mobile phone, e-mailing it to Twitpic is an efficient way to go. When you join Twitpic, you receive an exclusive e-mail address. From the Twitpic home page, click Settings to see your Twitpic e-mail address. Take a moment to input that e-mail address into your smartphone with the name Twitpic, that way it will always be at the ready.

6. You can track the images you upload by visiting your Twitpic home page. Your images appear in thumbnail form. If you want to delete one, just click the small trash-can next to the image. Click an individual thumbnail to access that photo's page. The URL of the photo page is the shortened link you can post anywhere on the Web to direct people to that image (in **Figure 13-13**, the URL is `http://twitpic.com/1nc16u`). Also, at the lower right on the photo page, you'll see a View counter that tells you how often your photo has been visited.

 When you sign in to Twitter, your computer stays signed in unless you sign out. When you first try to link another application to your Twitter account, you see a screen that asks you to allow the Web site to connect. This is a safe transaction, and the permissions will appear in your Twitter Settings: Connections area. If you want to disconnect from a service, you merely click the Revoke Access link for that service (see **Figure 13-14**).

Click here to disconnect a service.

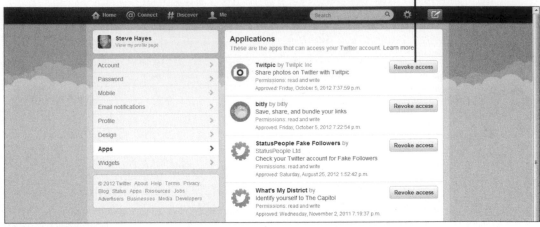

Figure 13-14

Become an Online Deejay (DJ)

1. I remember sitting around with my friends playing records, drinking wine, and having a great time. In today's so-very-busy world, we don't often have the opportunity to do that anymore. Oh yeah, there's also the fact that vinyl records have gone by the wayside, too. (Sigh.) But the Internet brings this all back to you when you visit blip.fm. Type **blip.fm** in your Web browser, and you come to the site's home page, as shown in **Figure 13-15**.

2. Joining is easy: Start by typing a DJ name in the Your DJ Name text box. You are known on the site by this name, so think twice about your selection. All your fiends will see this name when they visit the site, and it becomes the URL for your own Internet radio station. I kept it simple and used my Twitter name, MarshaCollier, so the URL for my blips is `http://blip.fm/MarshaCollier`.

3. Type your e-mail address in the Your Email Address text box and click the Sign Up button.

Figure 13-15

4. On the next page, you can connect your Twitter account by typing your Twitter username, so you can automatically post your songs (blips). After you add your Twitter account, you see a list of people you know from Twitter.

 I recommend that you click the box that unchecks all the check marks next to the proposed DJ list names. (Can you guess that my taste in music isn't heavy metal?) You can add favorite DJs later.

5. Next, connect to Facebook by selecting Facebook from the drop-down menu. You then see a Connect with Facebook button; click it. This connection occurs through Facebook Connect, which is an authentication service for sharing content. It's very similar to OAuth (see the preceding section), and it's safe.

6. You are now set up to post *blips* (your music selections) to both your Facebook and Twitter pages. In the next section, I show you how to toggle your posting status to either service or both. The default is both.

Spin Your Songs for Online Friends

1. You may ask, "What's a blip, *really*?" A *blip* is a combination of a song and a message that accompanies it. Why not create a blip now? Go to your DJ account at blip.fm (see the preceding section to set up an account, if you haven't), type the name of a song or artist in the Search box, and click Search.

2. You see a list of songs that blip.fm matches to your search. Click the Preview link on the right to listen to a song through your computer speakers. If the matched item is a video, you will see the video in the box to the right of the search results.

3. After you find the song you want to blip, click the word Blip (to the left of the title, as shown in **Figure 13-16**).

Click here for any song you want to blip.

Figure 13-16

4. A form similar to the one in **Figure 13-17** opens. Type a short message that you want to appear next to the blip's link in the Add a Message text box. As you type, notice that the countdown in the upper-right lets you know how many characters you have left.

Type a message.   See how many characters you have left.

Figure 13-17

5. Click the More Options link to expose the drop-down menu. From the menu, select the registered account where you want to post the blip. If you don't want to broadcast this to your Facebook account, click the Facebook icon and it will turn gray (which indicates that it won't post to Facebook). The Twitter icon still shows in blue.

6. Submitting a blip is also referred to as *blipping*, so click the Blip button and instantly the blip posts to your Twitter account. **Figure 13-18** shows you how it will appear.

MarshaCollier	**Name** Marsha Collier
	Location Los Angeles
	Web http://bit.ly/9h8skO
That's you!	**Bio** eBay For Dummies
☰ Lists ▾	series author / Host
	Computer & Technology
	Radio / Co-Founder
Thinking about my upcoming	#CustServ Chat /
South Beach vacation with a	Customer Service & Social
little Shakira ♫ http://blip.fm	Media Influencer / Fitness
/~qalpm	Nut
less than 20 seconds ago via Blip.fm	

16,773 17,611 937
following followers listed

Tweets   18,100

Favorites

Figure 13-18

Find and Share Videos on YouTube

Many more hours have been burned watching videos on YouTube
(www.youtube.com) than listening to songs on blip.fm. YouTube
bills itself as "Broadcast Yourself" so you'd think that you might find
only homemade videos. That's not the case. Big-time studios post portions of television shows and trailers from films. According to a study
from Comscore, in July 2012, the total number of videos viewed was
36.9 billion — and that's in *one* month! If you haven't visited the site,
you should.

 As of October 2012, the video that's had the all-time
most views — 785 million and counting — is *Baby*
from Justin Bieber and Ludacris. But, to prove that
popularity doesn't belong just to the big guys, the sev-
enth most popular (with over 485 million views) is
Charlie Bit My Finger Again. It's a short home movie
about an infant biting his older brother's finger, as
shown in **Figure 13-19**. Go figure. I guess there's a big
audience for kid videos; after all, the *Little Rascals* episodes are getting harder to find these days (unless you
look for a boxed set of DVDs on eBay).

1. To find a video to share, start by typing a keyword in the
search box on the home page at www.youtube.com.
You can search for topics, actors, singers, politicians . . .
just about anything. For example, I typed *Susan Boyle* (of

Britain's Got Talent fame) in the search box and got over 135,000 hits. And one of my favorite films is *One Six Right,* an independent film on the history of aviation. To find it, I type One Six Right into the text box and click Search. Try typing a search term for one of your favorites.

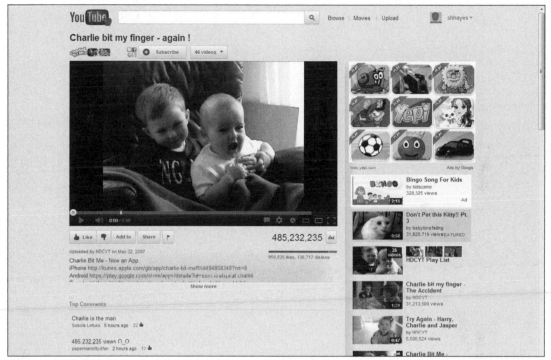

Figure 13-19

2. On the next page (the search results), you see a list of videos that match your search term. In my example, the videos have *One Six Right* in the title; I clicked the top one and came to the page shown in **Figure 13-20**.

3. To share a video that you find on YouTube, click the Share button that appears below the video viewing window. (Notice that e-mail, Twitter, and Facebook icons appear on the Share button.) A box opens on-screen, showing you the URL of the video and a collection of buttons that link to various online communities — including Facebook and Twitter.

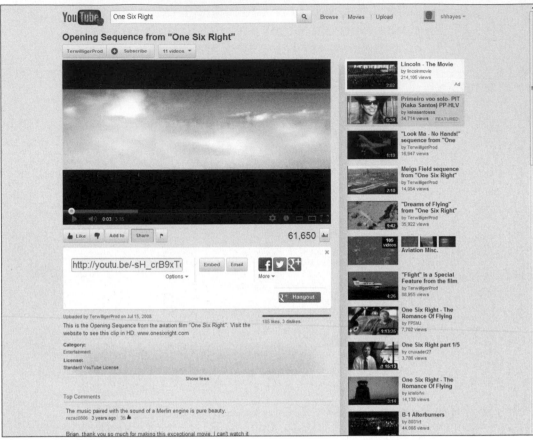

Figure 13-20

4. To share the video on Facebook, click the Facebook button; a window appears and offers you two ways to share:

    a. To post the video to your Facebook profile page, type your message in the text box and click the Share button. A box pops up giving you the option to post to many places. If you'd prefer to leave it on your Timeline, verify that the drop-down box above the text box says Share: On Your Own Timeline. **Figure 13-21** shows how it looks.

    b. If you'd prefer, you can send the video link as a message to a Facebook friend. Click the drop-down box next to Share and select In A Private Message. You then see a Facebook message window, as shown in **Figure 13-22**. Begin to type your Facebook friend's name, and a list will appear. Select your friend's name from this list, and the message is ready to send. Click Share Link to send it along to your friend's Facebook message center.

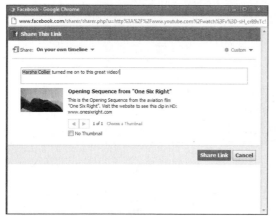

Figure 13-21

Type your friend's name here . . .   and select it here.

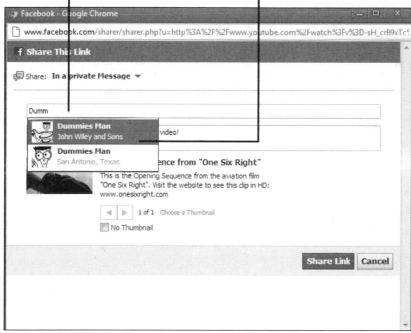

Figure 13-22

5. To share the video on Twitter, click the Twitter button and a second window opens with a message box containing the video's title and URL (see **Figure 13-23**). (If you're not signed in on Twitter, you need to do so and go back to YouTube and try again.) Edit the message if you'd rather say something other than the video's title, but don't delete the link. Click Tweet. Your message appears, along with the video URL, in your Twitter stream.

Figure 13-23

Giving or Taking an Opinion

Opinions are like bellybuttons — everybody has one. When you read reviews on the Web, realize that they can be written as honest evaluations — or they may be paid promotions (remember the payola scandals?) or slam jobs by the competition and spurned ex-employees. It takes a lot of reading to narrow down the wheat from the chaff.

The power of the Internet is that it's built on the voices of millions of people. The more people post reviews and give opinions, the more the truth on any topic will surface.

Crowd-sourcing is a popular 21st century form of marketing. When a company wants to learn about the consensus on a topic or product, it sends queries on the Internet and gleans data from the responses.

You know that the "wisdom of crowds" can sometimes be the opposite of wise. Members of a crowd can be too conscious of each other's opinions — so they begin to emulate the others' comments, which brings about conformity rather than a variety of views. We see that often these days, in political arguments on both sides of an issue.

Chapter 14

Get ready to . . .

➡ Check Out Angie's List 264

➡ Find Anything (and Its Reviews) on Amazon 265

➡ Find Restaurants, Shopping, and Nightlife on Yelp! 268

➡ Register on Yelp to Leave Reviews 270

➡ Leave a Review on Yelp..... 272

➡ Read Between the Lines at Review Sites 274

➡ Find Hotel Reviews on TripAdvisor 276

➡ Add a Hotel Review on TripAdvisor 278

➡ Find a Good Movie on Flixster 282

➡ Leave a Comment on Flixster 284

Speaking your mind on the Web is your chance to make a difference. All voices are weighted equally, and you can offer evaluations of products and services based on your experience. Plus, when you shop online, you can read the opinions of others on various sites to aide you in your personal buying decisions.

In this chapter, I show you some of the most popular sites where you can weigh in on your favorite products and businesses — and get advice when it comes to consumer purchases.

Check Out Angie's List

1. I'd like to start by mentioning an important site that I use frequently: Angies's List. *Angie's List* is a consumer review site that publishes user reviews on local service businesses and health providers. The site serves over 124 cities in the United States and provides reviews in more than 250 categories. Originally a site for local services, Angie's List has been gathering business reviews for close to 15 years and added medical industry provider reviews in 2008. Type **www.angieslist.com** in your browser's address bar and press Enter to reach the Angie's List home page, as shown in **Figure 14-1**.

2. Think about how much you might want to use a review site: You must be a paid member of Angie's List to view the member reviews. Angie's List compiles reviews for businesses and gives them grades in report card format. Just like in school, *A* is the highest grade, and *F* is the lowest. Along with the letter grades, members write descriptive reviews about their experiences with the businesses. I've been a member of Angie's List and have read reviews for several service businesses in my area.

3. You can't post anonymous reviews on Angie's List; the site expects its members to "take responsibility for their words." If someone posts a negative review about a business, Angie's List may contact the company in question to attempt to evaluate (and maybe correct) the situation that caused the bad review. At two places on the site — in its Membership Agreement and during report submission — the site states that it will share your report with the business being reviewed.

 Be advised: It's not necessarily cheap to be a member of Angie's List, and you can't find out how much it costs until you begin the sign-up process by setting up a username. I polled some people online and found that the pricing on membership subscriptions ranged from $10 to $70, and varied from city to city.

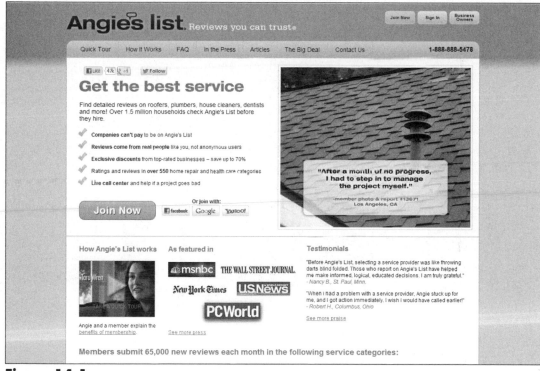

Figure 14-1

Find Anything (and Its Reviews) on Amazon

1. I must admit, I'm partial to Amazon. I've been shopping there since the site was launched in 1995. And now, Amazon is America's top online retailer. You can buy almost anything on Amazon, and almost every product has a long list of customer reviews.

 I read the reviews on Amazon even if I choose to buy an item elsewhere — although if the cost is only a few pennies different, I opt to shop at Amazon because of its incredible customer service.

2. Type **www.amazon.com** in your browser and press Enter. You arrive at the Amazon home page, as shown in **Figure 14-2**. At the top of the page is a search box where you can type in the name of any product: book, DVD, camera, cosmetic, tools, grocery items, and more. Click Go.

Type a product name here.   Click go.

Figure 14-2

3. Your search presents a new page containing a list of items that match your keywords. Click the name of the item you want to read reviews about, and you arrive at the product page.

4. To get to the reviews, click the number of customer reviews just below the title at the top of the product page.

Figure 14-3 shows that you'll find 12 customer reviews for this product.

Click here for customer reviews.

Figure 14-3

5. When you arrive at the reviews page (see **Figure 14-4**), you first see the most helpful favorable review and the most helpful critical review. Reviews are even reviewed by users of the site, so valuable reviews are often pushed to the top — and reviews without value get pushed to the bottom. Scroll down the page to see more reviews.

Customer Reviews
eBay For Dummies (For Dummies (Computer/Tech))

12 Reviews		Average Customer Review	Search Customer Reviews
5 star:	(8)	★★★★☆ (12 customer reviews)	[ ] GO
4 star:	(3)	Share your thoughts with other customers	☑ Only search this product's reviews
3 star:	(1)	Create your own review	
2 star:	(0)		
1 star:	(0)		

The most helpful favorable review | **The most helpful critical review**

6 of 6 people found the following review helpful

★★★★★ **Great source of knowledge!**
I've wanted to sell on eBay for years but felt intimidated by the prospect. I've bought off eBay literally hundreds of times, yet this book taught me more helpful clues to better buying than I thought existed. Now I have the confidence to begin to sell on eBay because of reading (and then rereading) this book. I definitely recommend it to anyone who is new to eBay...
Read the full review ›
Published 4 months ago by Rebecca S. Evans

Vs.

★★★☆☆ **Not so much for dummies.**
This book was definitely not for dummies! There was so much info that my head was swimming, and it was so "nit-picky". If a person is more computer-savvy than I am, it would probably be ok, but it wasn't the case for me. My granddaughter taught me more about selling on eBay than the book did.
Published 5 days ago by bluebonnet gal

See more 3 star, 2 star, 1 star reviews

Figure 14-4

Find Restaurants, Shopping, and Nightlife on Yelp!

I think I was one of the first users of Yelp. I love the service — and even have its mobile application on my phone so I can check out restaurants while I'm on the run. I also use Yelp when I plan a vacation to check out the facilities close to where I'm staying.

1. Founded in 2004 by software engineers (formerly from PayPal), Yelp now receives approximately 78 million visits per month from seekers of local business reviews. You do not need to register on the site to search reviews or get the special deals and coupons offered by the businesses on the site. Type **www.yelp.com** into your Web browser, and you arrive at a Yelp home page for your closest metro area.

In **Figure 14-5** the home page I see brings me to Los Angeles. I checked with a group of people on Twitter (crowd-sourcing) and found that *most* people got their cities pre-filled-in on the home screen. A few people in Seattle, New Jersey, and Iowa came up with San Francisco on their home page, so the little program that fills in the city is clearly not an exact science yet. If your city (or the city you wish to search in) isn't listed, just type your ZIP code (or city and state) in the box below Near. You'll be brought to the hub for that city.

2. If you want to browse businesses in the area, just click one of the links to Refine By. To refine your search further (by ratings, location, features, or prices), click the Show Filters arrow — a drop-down box with more options appears. Clicking a category (for example, *restaurants*) brings a dizzying array of results. In this case, narrowing down the results to a type of food gives you a more manageable list.

Type a location here.

Figure 14-5

 Yelp sells advertising to local businesses, and advertisers on Yelp get preferred placement in the search results and the extra listing features. If you see top listing results that are highlighted, this means those listed businesses are paid advertisers.

3. To search directly for a type of business, type the keyword in the search box, followed by the name of the city you want to search in. For example, I typed *veterinarian Huntington Beach California* in the search box. Then I selected a listing and clicked it (because I saw a notation that this business has a Special Offer in the listing). **Figure 14-6** shows the business page and the offer.

Animal Care Center Of Huntington Beach

★★★★★ 5 reviews 📊 Rating Details

Like •

Add Photos

Category: Veterinarians [Edit]

8851 Adams Ave
Huntington Beach, CA 92646

(714) 962-3639
www.acchb.com

📨 **First new client exam free!**
We're so sure you'll love us and yelp all about it
that we offer free first exams for all new clients
with the purchase of any other service

Hours:
Mon-Tue, Thu-Fri 8 a.m. - 6
p.m.
Sat 8 a.m. - 1 p.m.

📝 Edit Business Info

🏆 First to Review 📷 leslie k.

📧 Send to Friend   📑 Bookmark   📱 Send to Phone   📝 Write a Review   🖨 Print

Special Offer Nearby   Sponsored Result

View Larger Map/Directions »

Browse Nearby:
Restaurants | Nightlife | Shopping |
Movies | All

**People Who Viewed This Also
Viewed...**

Huntington Pet Vet
★★★★★ 13 reviews
Huntington Beach, CA

Brookfield Pet Hospital...
★★★★★ 2 reviews
Fountain Valley, CA

Gill A DVM
★★★★★ 1 review
Huntington Beach, CA

Figure 14-6

4. When you view a business listing page on Yelp, you may
notice a competitive paid ad at the top of that business's
page. Be sure to scroll down to read the reviews (see
Figure 14-7).

👍 0
👎 2

leslie k.
Huntington
Beach, CA

★★★★★ 3/20/2008

Great Vet. Today, we took our 3 month old puppy to see Dr. Hill and she
was great. My puppy really liked her and wanted to talk to here about a
bunch of stuff. Barking excitedly about her new life with her family, I hope.
The Doctor was informative and took the time to talk to us about our dog
and what to expect later in the development process. The tech people were
wonderful and nice. Even the clients were great. If you aren't sure about
your vet, give ACCHB a try. You will be happy you did.

Was this review Useful •   Funny •   Cool •

🔖 Bookmark 📧 Send to a Friend 🔗 Link to This Review   💬 Add owner comment

Figure 14-7

Register on Yelp to Leave Reviews

1. If you want to leave a review for a business, you must
register on Yelp. On any Yelp page, click the Sign up for
Yelp link. You find yourself looking at a simple registration form where you type your name, e-mail address, and

ZIP code, and select a password. The form asks your gender and birth dates, but you needn't fill it in; that information is optional.

2. Next you arrive at a page where Yelp wants you to find your e-mail contacts that are on the site. You are asked to input your e-mail login and password as shown in **Figure 14-8**. Then Yelp logs in to your online contact list to see whether anyone on your list matches with current Yelp members. I'm not a fan of letting anyone know who my contacts are, even though doing so (in this case) is safe. If you squint really hard, you can see an inconspicuous Skip This Step link next to the Find Friends button. Why not click it?

Are your friends here?
Find friends you email from Yahoo! Mail, Gmail, Hotmail, AOL, and other email services.

Your Email Address   sue@aol.com
                          (e.g. bob@yahoo.com)

Your Email Password

                          (The password you use to log into your email)

🔒 **Your Information is Safe**
We don't store your email password.
Your email password is used to find your friends on Yelp.

                          Skip this step   Find Friends

Figure 14-8

3. A Welcome page greets you and offers you several options. Click Please Complete Your Yelp Registration to get to a page where you assign yourself a nickname for the site. Or you may click the Go to My Profile button where you also can fill in your nickname, as well as upload your photo and personalize your profile — as little or as much as you wish. Mine is pretty jazzy, as shown in **Figure 14-9**.

4. In the meantime, Yelp sends you an e-mail to confirm your e-mail address. It will have a link in it, when you click it; you end up back on Yelp where you confirm that your e-mail is correct.

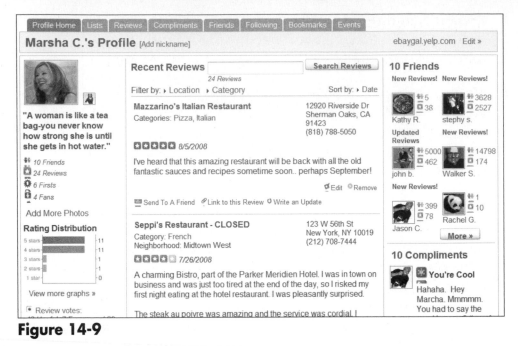

Figure 14-9

Leave a Review on Yelp

1. Every page on Yelp has a navigation bar with links to various areas on the site. Click any of those links to get to your desired area. To post a review, find the Write a Review link and click it. You land on a search page. Type the name of the business and city in the Business Name and Near text boxes, and click the Search Businesses button, as shown in **Figure 14-10**.

Figure 14-10

2. Scroll through the group of loosely related listings to find the exact business you're searching for. Click the matching business name to get to its page. Click the Write a Review link on the mini-navigation bar just below the business details (and above the reviews).

3. On the Complete Your Review page, you see the review form on the left — and other folks' reviews of the business on the right. On the review form, put your mouse pointer over the stars to select the star ranking you wish to give (one to five), and click your selection.

4. Type your review in the text box, as shown in **Figure 14-11**. Scroll down the page and optionally add an evaluation of whether you feel the photos of the business give a good representation, and click from one to four dollar signs to give others an idea of the pricing of the product or services you've received.

5. When you're done, click Post. Your review appears on Yelp for all to see — and on your About Me Profile page. From your profile, you can update a review at any time.

Complete Your Review of C the Salon - Studio City, CA 91604

Rating ⭐⭐⭐⭐⭐ *Woohoo! As good as it gets!*

Your Review

Read our review guidelines

I've been getting my hair done here for five years now. If you're looking for a colorist/stylist that truly understands redheads, ask for Patty. She only works a few days a week as she has a regular job styling for television. When Patty isn't available, I've also had Claudio do my hair and been very happy.

Auto-saved a moment ago (9:50pm).

Figure 14-11

Read Between the Lines at Review Sites

1. Travel-booking sites such as TripAdvisor list thousands of restaurants, hotels, and other businesses, which can make choosing among them daunting when you're searching for a hotel or restaurant in a particular city. You may want to try alternative search methods to adjust the results you get:

- Use an Internet search engine (such as Google) to narrow down your results. You can search for a specific city name and facility — or a desired service — to get a smaller list of results.

- If you're looking for deals from hotels or airlines, also visit www.bing.com/travel to widen your choices. Bing scours many different travel sites to get results based on price and ratings. After you find a few possibilities this way, then go to these sites to read the reviews.

2. While you're reading reviews, keep in mind that conditions someone else considers dreadful may not bother you at all. Here are a couple of examples:

- A friend of mine booked a trip on the east coast using Bing travel and TripAdvisor. When she and her friend arrived in a lovely hotel in Manhattan, her friend couldn't stop grousing about how small the room was. (If you've ever stayed in a New York City Hotel room, you know that almost anything over closet size is acceptable.)

- I recently booked a lovely hotel just off the Champs d'Élysées in Paris. The bulk of the reviews on TripAdvisor didn't come from happy campers. I figured at least the reviews said the room was clean and I was willing to pay the premium to stay at the location. When I arrived, I found that the small hotel was just lovely, and I was very pleased. (Of course, I knew to expect that a hotel in Paris might not have the same amenities expected from a hotel in the United States.)

3. Clearly, if you discover a hotel with a *bunch* of bad reviews, like the one shown in **Figure 14-12**, you might want to steer clear of that property.

> **❝ Hotel Hell ❞**
>
> ◉○○○○
> U_____ff2 ▼ 2 contributions
> PA
>
> Mar 13, 2010 | Trip type: Friends getaway
>
> a bunk bed in a closet.... you have to share the bathroom with the whole floor!! we looked at the room and didnt want to stay and they wouldnt refund our money. your better off sleeping in a dirty cardboard box. more
>
> 📷 1 Photo

Save Review

Figure 14-12

Keep an eye out for extra information associated with a review. I noticed that the review for the hotel in **Figure 14-12** also included a photo, so I decided to click it. I saw what you can see in **Figure 14-13**. Yep, you guessed it: I'm not paying $130 a night for that. Really!

the whole room!!! filthy dive
From Review: Hotel Hell on Mar 2010, (U_____ff2)

Figure 14-13

4. Individual tastes in restaurants can also vary widely. One of my favorite restaurants serves very small portions, and I love that. Others might post a review complaining that the portion size is too small. Bottom line? Use your good sense and read between the lines when you're reading any reviews.

Find Hotel Reviews on TripAdvisor

TripAdvisor is one of the most popular travel sites on the Web, netting almost 38 million visitors a month. Having so many visitors gives this site's reviews a lot more clout. If a hotel or restaurant has two reviews on one site, a visit to TripAdvisor might net 23 reviews; which would you prefer? This site currently has over 75 million independent reviews.

1. Finding hotel information in TripAdvisor is easy. Type the URL **www.tripadvisor.com** into your Web browser address box, press Enter, and you arrive at the home page shown in **Figure 14-14**. You'll see you have several options.

2. In the Plan the Perfect Trip box, you can get immediate targeted information. Type in the city you're visiting and click the Find Hotels button. A results page shows up with full results for those dates and location.

3. Refine your search. On the top and left side of the page are options you can set to best suit your needs. You can always change these in mid-search should you not find something suitable that fits your parameters. Pare down your selections by using the qualifiers in this list:

- **Check availability:** Enter the dates you plan to travel along with the number of adults in your party.

- **Price per night:** Check the box showing how much you've budgeted per night for your hotel stay.

- **Property type:** Are you more of a hotel person or is a quaint bed and breakfast more to your liking? This section lets you narrow down to your preference.

- **Neighborhood:** If there are nearby areas that might be acceptable, you have your choice of selecting them.

- **Traveler rating:** Define how highly rated a hotel you want to find. This rating is based on the independent reviews posted to the site. If a one- or two-bullet hotel (they use bullet points instead of stars) is not where you want to stay, use the slider to remove them from the results.

Figure 14-14

- **Hotel class:** Here's where the star ratings come in. You may select All or any combination of one star to five stars. If you only want to stay in a four-star or five-star property, you can select both for your results.

- **Amenities:** You require a fitness center? Check it off! Select from amenities such as parking, swimming pools, room service, free Internet, pets allowed, and more. Select as many as you like.

- **Property name:** Did you get a recommendation from a friend and want to see what others have to say? Type the hotel name in here to go directly to its reviews.

- **Hotel brand:** If you're looking for a specific chain of hotels, you can select it here.

With a little tinkering and the use of your good common sense, you'll be able to find a hotel that meets your needs.

Add a Hotel Review on TripAdvisor

1. Adding a hotel review on TripAdvisor is an easy task. After you come back from your trip and have an opinion to share, here's how you can share it with the world. First you must register in order to submit your review and post it on the site. You can register before or after you write your review.

2. You have two ways to register, as shown in **Figure 14-15**.

    a. If you've already set up a Facebook account, you can sign in to TripAdvisor using your Facebook login details. This method is safe — and the easiest way to join. To join via Facebook Connect (a service that allows you to keep your login info and passwords to a minimum), click the Sign In with Facebook button. If you're not already signed in to Facebook, you have to sign in at this point.

Sign up for TripAdvisor

Sign up using your Facebook account (Recommended) -
Why?

f Sign in with Facebook

The easier way to sign in to TripAdvisor

...or fill out the form below

E-mail address

Already a TripAdvisor
member?

Choose your password

Sign in

Pick a screen name

Current city

☑ Keep me signed in on this computer

Sign up

Figure 14-15

b. *If you haven't set up a Facebook account, you can create a
   TripAdvisor account by supplying your e-mail address and
   choosing a password.* Just pick a screen name and password and tell the site what city you live in. Then click
   Sign Up, and you're a member!

3. Find the page for the property you want to review on
   TripAdvisor by searching the hotel name and city. When
   the results appear, click the link to the hotel you wish to
   review, as shown in **Figure 14-16**. Then follow the rest of
   the steps given here as you write a review.

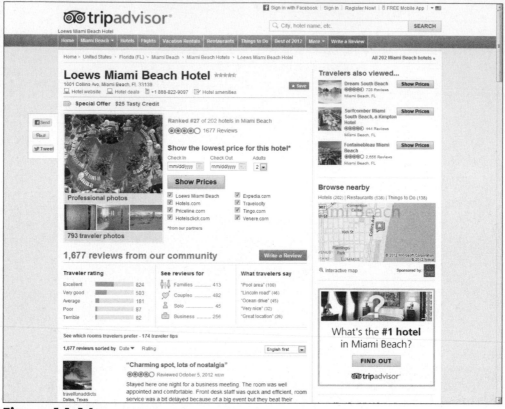

Figure 14-16

4. Choose one of the two places to click to enter the *Write a Review* form. Click the top navigation bar or the area to the right with the user's ratings. Clicking either one takes you to a form like the one in **Figure 14-17**.

5. The name of the property will already be on the top of the page, and the first thing to do is fill out the overall rating of one to five bullets. Now it's time to write your review.

6. Type in a title, describing the hotel in one sentence. In the Your Review text box, type your observations. Tell what you liked and what you didn't like about your stay. (Your review has to be at least 200 characters long.)

7. In the What Sort of Trip Was This? area, select the option that best describes your reason for travel, ranging from business to solo. The When Did You Travel? section asks you to narrow your travel dates down to the month and year of your visit.

8. The Could You Say a Little More About It section is an optional portion of the review that lets you assign specific ratings to several important factors, including Service, Value, and Cleanliness. This section is an important stop if you found some parts of the hotel to your liking while others were lacking. There's also a text box where you can add a tip on the best rooms on the property.

9. Optionally, upload a photo. If you've taken a photo of the hotel or its property that you'd like to share, click the *Browse* button and upload it from your computer. You also must check the box stating that the photo is yours and that you're not infringing on anyone's rights by posting it.

Figure 14-17

10. Since TripAdvisor takes the reviews very seriously, you must check the box next to the statement that assures: "I certify that this review is my own experience and is my genuine opinion of this hotel, and that I have no personal or business affiliation with this establishment, and have not been offered any incentive or payment originating from the establishment to write this review."

11. When you're pleased with your work, click Submit your review. After you submit your review, it appears in your profile, marked as pending. All reviews are checked before posting; it usually takes a few days before they appear. When your review is posted, you'll receive an e-mail confirmation. If TripAdvisor chooses not to post your review, the site sends you an e-mail and lets you know the reason why.

Find a Good Movie on Flixster

1. Flixster is a social site where you can read movie reviews, get local movie show times, watch trailers, and post your own comments about films. You arrive at the Flixster home page by typing **www.flixster.com** in your browser's address bar and pressing Enter. **Figure 14-18** shows you the home page where you can access a lot of information.

2. To get to the various location on the site, use the drop-down menus from the navigation bar. Also on the navigation bar, you get a search box in the upper-right corner where you can replace the *Movies*, *Actors*, *Directors* text by typing the appropriate title or name. Then click Search.

3. Farther down the page, as **Figure 14-19** shows, is the area where you can click tabs to view the specific selections: Top Box Office hits, movies that are Opening soon, and New DVDs released. Clicking any film title takes you to the film's hub page that includes a trailer, photos from the film, the reviews from published critics, and comments left by members of the site.

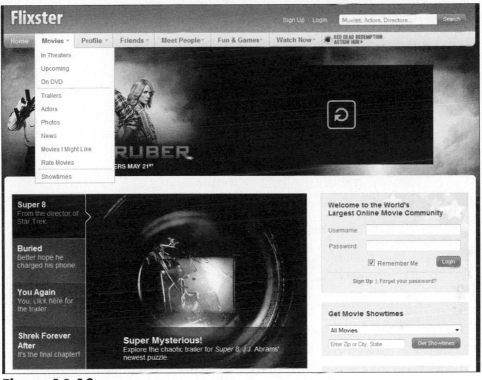

Figure 14-18

Figure 14-19

Leave a Comment on Flixster

1. To post your opinion (after you've seen the film, of course), you've got to register on the Flixster site (`www.flixster.com`). There's no Facebook Connect offered here, so you must create a new account. Click the Sign Up link in the upper-right corner of the page and the registration form appears (as shown in **Figure 14-20**).

2. To register, supply your name, e-mail address, gender, and birth date. You may click the check box that says *Hide my age* — that way, it won't appear on your Profile page.

3. Then select a password and type the words from the Captcha code into the text box.

4. If you don't want to receive weekly e-mail messages from Flixster, uncheck the default check mark that you find in the box next to the words *Send me a weekly update*. Recognize that when you click the Join Flixster button, you're agreeing to the Terms of Service (TOS) for the site. You can't join if you don't agree. And after you're a member, you can go to any film's hub page to leave a comment on the film.

Figure 14-20

So You Want to Be a Blogger?

Chapter
15

You've heard about blogs, right? Even the learned sage Homer (Simpson) commented, "Instead of one big shot controlling all the media, now there's a thousand freaks Xeroxing their worthless opinions." Maybe not so learned, but he's more or less right — except those opinions are now online, in the millions, and are (some of them, anyway) actually worth reading. Having your own blog gives you an opportunity to write about things that interest you and add your opinions to the social buzz — and someone will probably read what you write!

Once you get involved on Twitter and Facebook, you'll see your friends linking to blog *posts* (online journal entries) and news stories. Doing a blog post is so much more personal because each one is filled with your opinions and your information.

In this chapter, I show you how to set up a blog on the Web at no cost (that means free), and give you examples of people just like you who are blogging on the Web.

Get ready to. . .

⟶ Answer These Questions Before You Start.............. 286

⟶ Stake Your Claim in the Blogosphere 288

⟶ Register Your Blog............. 289

⟶ Give Your Blog a Name 291

⟶ Post Your Story with Photos...................... 293

⟶ Set Up Your Profile............ 300

Answer These Questions Before You Start

I've learned from experience that before I begin any project, I need to define some parameters that guide the project path and clarify the desired result. If you begin your blog with a plan, the blogging habit will become a pleasure rather than a chore.

1. **Who are you?** In your blog you'll have a profile. Be prepared to talk about your business background, your family, your hobbies, and even life lessons you've learned. Think about sharing pictures and videos in the future. The more information you're willing to share, the more inclined readers will be to invest time in reading your words.

2. **Why you are blogging?** If you spell out your purpose for blogging, your intentions will be clear. Are you writing for your children or grandchildren? Are you writing for your contemporaries to share thoughts? Are you writing to connect with a business community and to promote your online business (and if you're buying and selling on eBay, did you read my book *eBay For Dummies* from Wiley)? These are all valid reasons to blog. But know that if your purpose is to promote an online business, today's successful marketing is fueled by being a real person on the Web and building a social community.

 As Mack Collier (one of the nation's premier business blog experts) says, "Consider your audience when answering this question, ask yourself, 'Why would someone come to this blog, what would they be looking for?'" (Hint: Your visitors won't be coming to your blog just so you can make a pitch to them.) Visit Mack's blog for good tips at www.mackcollier.com.

3. **What will you blog about?** You can blog about any subject you wish — including your family, your hobbies, your politics . . . when it comes to blogging, you're limited only by your imagination! Just let your readers know what's up so they know what to expect. In **Figure 15-1**, I show you the header of my blog. (If you'd like to check out my blog, you'll find it at `mcollier.blogspot.com`).

Marsha Collier's Musings

I'm the author of the "For Dummies" series of books about eBay and **Customer Service**, Host of **Computer and Technology Radio**. I blog on eBay, useful products and anything fun. Also please visit my eBay book website **Cool eBay Tools**

Figure 15-1

My blog header is purposefully innocuous because I cover so many different things. I write about my books, business, family, my garden, and my life! Stay focused and think of the header as a "mission statement" for your future blog posts.

Jessica Gottlieb, Queen of the Mommy Bloggers, had a simple statement header that appeared on every page of her blog before she redesigned (see **Figure 15-2**). I loved it because when you read it, you immediately know who she is and where she's coming from.

Jessica Gottlieb
Wife. Writer. Mother. Friend.

Figure 15-2

Visit her updated blog at `www.jessicagottlieb.com` and you may be shocked by her candid posts. She's very outspoken; named a Power Mom by Nielsen in 2008 and 2009, and averages 43,000 unique visitors each month.

4. **What will you do to get people to your blog?** Visit other people's blogs and leave comments. To find blogs from people of like mind, go to Google and search for a topic. In **Figure 15-3**, I searched for *gardening*. Then, on the left side of the page, I clicked Blogs and Past Week in the toolbar to find the most recent posts.

Choose blogs.   Type a topic here.

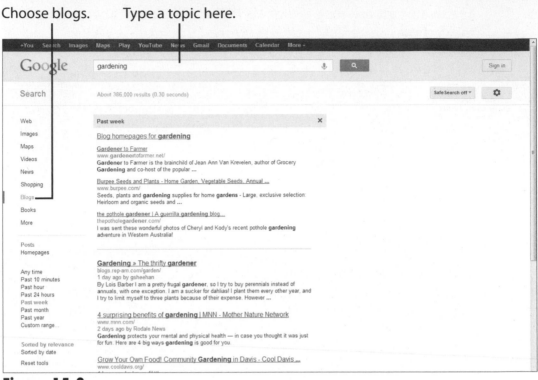

Figure 15-3

Visit, read, and comment on blogs that interest you — even ask questions to promote conversation. Other readers (as well as the blogger) may reply and click over to check out your blog. If you see a post that's on a similar topic to something you've posted on, suggest people check your blog.

5. **How do you get your audience to come back?** Expect (okay, *hope*) that people will leave comments on your posts. Be sure to comment back and visit their blogs. It's all about interacting with the blogging community. One hand washes the other . . . .

Stake Your Claim in the Blogosphere

1. Time to take the first step: Sign up at a site that will *host* (provide an online home for) your blog. Starting off at a

site that won't ask for payment is a nice idea, and Google fits that bill. Since 2003, Google Blogger has hosted Web sites for anyone who wants to join in the world of blogging. The only caveat is that you need to have a Google account.

2. If you use any of Google's services, you probably have an account already. If not, flip to Chapter 3: All About E-Mail to find the steps for getting a Google account by setting up an e-mail account with Google's Gmail service. Google Gmail is the most popular free e-mail service on the Web; that's mainly because of large (and free!) online storage space and excellent spam filters. When you set it up, you'll be able to handle your e-mail on the gmail. com Web site, or make it so the mail gets downloaded to almost any e-mail program on your computer.

 After you create a Google account, you get access to all of Google when you sign in to Google services and set up your blog.

Register Your Blog

1. Now it's time to jump in. Go to www.blogger.com and sign in by typing your Google username (e-mail address) and password where prompted, as shown in **Figure 15-4**. Then click Sign In.

2. When you arrive at the Confirm Your Profile form, your name is already filled in, as shown in **Figure 15-5**. You have a couple options for how to set up your blog. The default option is to tie the blog to a Google+ profile. Google+ is a social network, similar to Facebook, but operated by Google and integrated into their services. If you'd prefer to post under a different name, you can click the Switch to a Limited Blogger Profile link and use whatever name you wish.

Figure 15-4

Figure 15-5

Because we don't cover Google+ in this book and for the sake of simplicity, I recommend you use the limited profile option. You can still use your real name if you wish.

If you'd like to find out more about Google+, look for *Google+ For Dummies* at your local bookstore or favorite online book seller.

3. Click the Switch to a Limited Blogger Profile link and fill in your Display Name. That's the name that Blogger uses automatically every time you sign your posts. Make it easy for your friends to know who you are — use your own name. I used to go by *cre8ive* and none of my friends knew that I was commenting on their blogs!

4. Click the Continue to Blogger link to move on to the steps for setting up and launching your blog.

Give Your Blog a Name

Now that you've agreed to join the masses of people who are spilling their hearts and souls (and, in some cases, guts) on the Internet, it's time to name the baby.

1. Click the New Blog button. A new window pops up with options for naming your blog, establishing an address, and selecting a template for how your blog will look.

2. Name your blog. This title will appear on your Dashboard and on the blog pages. Don't freak out and freeze up at this point! You can change the name of your blog at any time. So go easy on yourself.

3. Give your blog a Web address (URL). Okay, this gets a little sticky. You can change this part later, but the URL you select becomes the Web address for your blog. It's what people must type in their browsers when they want to go to your blog.

Because there are a lot of Blogger blogs, Google scans to make sure that your URL is available and alerts you when it isn't. (see **Figure 15-6**).

Google lets you know if the URL you want for your blog is available.

Figure 15-6

4. You have the option to choose a template for your blog. Choosing a template is no big deal — you can always change it later. You can also make simple changes to the template — say, placement of columns and colors and such. If you're technically inclined, you can even create your own custom template after your blog is set up. But for now, you've got to pick one — so scroll through the available templates. If you'd like to start with a very basic blog, choose the one called Simple to start.

5. When you're all set up, click the Create blog! button. You're taken to a screen, shown in **Figure 15-7** that allows you to manage your blog, including options to make your first post.

Figure 15-7

In the future, you can purchase a custom URL (that is, a Web address you specify) from Google and use it for your blog. It currently costs about $10 per year. Wait until your blog evolves to see whether you want to continue with it. Once you've purchased a URL, that's it — no changing your mind.

Post Your Story with Photos

Posting to you blog is as easy as using a word processor. The New Post page (**Figure 15-8**) has everything you need.

Type your post text here. Use text formatting tools.   Preview your blog posts.

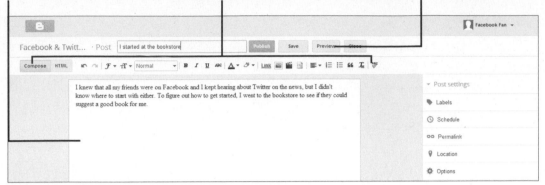

Figure 15-8

1. Give your post a title: Make your title catchy, with key-words that reflect the topic.

2. Write your post: Compose your blog post in the text area. Use the toolbar to change the formatting of your text if you wish. Use bold, italic, colors, or numbering — just as in a word processing program.

> Don't use a word-processing program if you pre-write your post. I know spell checking is handy, but when it comes time to copy and paste what you've written, some of the characters won't transfer properly. If you want to pre-write, use a plain "text editor" program like Notepad.

If you're writing your post in Blogger, don't worry about having to hurry. Take your time. Blogger autosaves your work every few minutes.

3. Add a picture. People love pictures! Click the icon of the photo in the toolbar (**Figure 15-9**). You're brought to another page (**Figure 15-10**) where you can upload a photo from a number of sources.

- **Upload:** This choice lets you select a photo saved to your computer. Click the Choose Files button to browse your computer's memory for the photo you want.

Click here to add a picture.

Figure 15-9

Upload a file from these sources.

Figure 15-10

- **From this blog:** After you've added a few posts and photos, you may find yourself wanting to reuse some photos you previously posted to the blog. This option offers a quick way to repost older images.

- **From Picasa Web Albums:** Picasa is Google's photo storing and sharing service. It's tied to their photo editing software, also called Picasa, you can download for free. After you've established a Google account, you can add a Picasa album to your mix.

- **From your phone:** Mobile phones are replacing cameras as the most popular option for shooting quick photos. This option lets you grab a photo from your phone and add it to a blog post.

- **From your webcam:** Can you think of a better way to personalize a blog post than by adding a photo of you creating the post? If your computer is equipped with a webcam, a device that lets you shoot images with your computer, then you can shoot and add one automatically.

- **From a URL:** When inserting a photo, you can type in the Web address (URL) for an image elsewhere on the Web. Before you "liberate" a photo from another Web site, be sure it's not a copyrighted image: Check Chapter 13, where I talk about Creative Commons and copyright issues.

4. The photos you've added appear in the Select a File box as they're uploaded to Google. Select the image you want to add to your blog post and click the Add Selected button (see **Figure 15-11**).

 You can add multiple images with a single click. Simply select the images you want to add to the post and click the Add Selected button when you have the set you want.

5. Blogger drops your image into your post wherever you left your cursor after you were finished with the text (see **Figure 15-12**). If you don't like where it's sitting or the size of the image, you can change it.

6. To move your image, hover your cursor over the image until it turns into a cross-arrow. Left click and hold the button. You can now move the image around in the post. Release the button when the image lands where you want it to live in the post.

Select the image you want to add . . .   then click this button

Figure 15-11

Figure 15-12

7. If you want to resize your image or add a caption, click the image to bring up an options menu (shown in **Figure 15-13**). You have the option to automatically resize the image to Small, Medium, Large, X-Large, or original size. Click through your options to see which fits best in the post. The menu also gives you options to move the image to a specific place in the post or add a caption.

Choose a size and location for the photo.

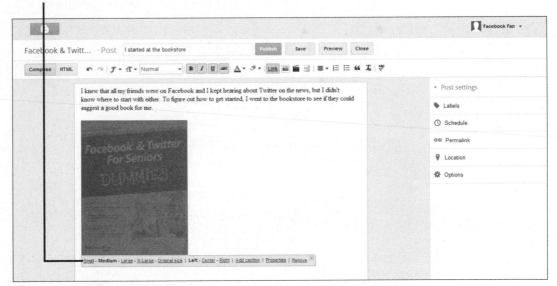

Figure 15-13

8. After you've added all the text and images you want to add to a post, click Preview to see how the finished product will appear on your blog. A new window (shown in **Figure 15-14**) pops up to show you what the world will see when they visit your blog.

Figure 15-14

9. If your post is ready and you want to put it live on the Web, click Publish. If you'd rather give it extra thought, just click Save and it goes into your posting area. Click Close after you've saved if you want to shut your post down before you revisit. Once you're ready to finish, you can find the post on your Dashboard (see **Figure 15-15**) in the Drafts link under Posts. You can add to or edit the post at any time.

Find your unpublished post here.

Figure 15-15

Set Up Your Profile

You can't have a blog without a profile. You lose a lot of credibility when people can't put at a face to the blog. Some people don't use their own photos and, instead, use avatars to remain anonymous. Perhaps they don't like the photos they have of themselves, and an avatar is fine to use. But you do need to offer a little background about yourself. After all, your readers can't always relate to you without some idea of who you are.

1. To set up your profile on your blog, click the Blogger logo at the top of the page to return to the Dashboard. You arrive at your blog's Dashboard, as shown in **Figure 15-16**. Find your display name in the upper right and click it to open the drop-down menu.

Click here to go to your profile.

Figure 15-16

2. Click the Blogger profile link. You arrive at a screen showing your current profile. Unless you've already added info to your profile, this page should be pretty sparse (**Figure 15-17**), with only your display name and blogs listed. Click the Edit Profile button in the upper right to start updating your profile.

Click this to start updating your profile.

Figure 15-17

3. Most of the questions are self-explanatory, and pretty benign. A few are important to fill out on your first pass — especially these:

- **Share my profile:** Clicking the box here makes your profile page appear as a link from your blog; it puts a face on the words in the blog.

- **Show my e-mail address:** I recommend declining to check this box. People can comment on your blog and Blogger will send the comments in the form of e-mails to your Gmail account. Showing your e-mail address only invites spam.

- **Profile photo:** There's an option to either upload a picture from your computer or to use a photo that's already on the Web. If you want to put in a photo from the Web, just type in the URL of the photo in the text box (as in **Figure 15-18**) and the second you finish typing it in, it will magically appear on the page.

Click here if you want to use a photo from the Web.

Type the URL of the photo you want to use.

Profile Photo

◉ From your computer:
Choose File No file chosen

○ From the web. Paste an image URL below.

Figure 15-18

If you want to upload an image from your computer, click the Choose File button to open a window to your hard drive, navigate to the folder where you store the very best photos of yourself, and Double-click the photo. In a moment, it appears on the profile page.

4. Fill in whatever else suits your fancy and, when you're done, click the Save Profile button at the bottom of the page. Your Edit User Profile page reappears, bearing the reassurance that *Your settings have been saved*. To view your profile, click the View Updated Profile link and you see the fruits of your labor, as shown in **Figure 15-19**.

Figure 15-19

Index

• *Symbols and Numerics* •

@ sign
  about, 43
  used in Facebook, 133
  used in Twitter, 204–205
/ (forward slash), 220
(hashtags), 209, 226–230
2.4GHz band, 37–39
5GHz band, 38–39
802.11a, 38
802.11b, 38, 39
802.11g, 38, 39
802.11n, 38–39

• *A* •

accessing
  Hotmail, 48
  Yahoo! Mail, 47
accounts
  Facebook, 80–82, 90
  Gmail, 52–57
  Twitter, 194–197
adding
  contacts to Gmail, 57–59
  hotel reviews on TripAdvisor, 278–281
  personal information to Facebook, 84–85
  photos to Timeline in Facebook, 111–112
  Timeline events in Facebook, 112–113
  yourself to WeFollow, 221–222
adjusting Twitter account settings, 194–197
administrator for groups (Facebook), 167
Adobe Flash Player, 140
age, on Facebook, 81
AIM (AOL Instant Messenger) feature, 46
albums (photo), creating on Facebook, 141–145
Amazon, 19, 265–267
#americanidol chat, 228
Angie's List, 264–265
AOL Instant Messenger (AIM) feature, 46
Application Directory (Facebook), 176
apps (Facebook), 154, 174–179
asking questions on Twitter, 212
Asus Seashell, 14
@ sign
  about, 43
  used in Facebook, 133
  used in Twitter, 204–205
Atom processor, 17
avatars, uploading, 197–198

• B •

backward-compatible, 38
BestBuy.com (website), 19
Bing (website), 274
bit.ly, 246
blip, defined, 256
blip.fm, 254–258
#blogchat chat, 228
Blogger (Google), 289
blogging
  about, 285
  naming your blog, 291–293
  planning, 286–288
  posting your story with photos,
    293–300
  registering blogs, 289–291
  setting up profiles, 300–303
  signing up for blogs, 288–289
BlogSpot, 71–72
broadband connection
  about, 28–30
  choosing, 32–34
Brogan, Chris (blogger), 242
browsers, 12, 21–26
browsing Facebook, 176–179
Buy.com (website), 19

• C •

cable connection, 30
Calendar (Google), 50
calendars, exporting Facebook
    Events to, 173–174
Captcha codes, 56, 187
#carchat chat, 228
case sensitivity, in Twitter searches,
    209

CD/DVD drive, 18
central processing unit (CPU), 17
#CES hashtag, 226
Chat (Google), 49
chats
  Facebook, 130–132
  Twitter, 228–229
Chefville, 179
choosing
  broadband connection, 32–34
  hardware, 12–16
  ISP (Internet Service Provider),
    28–31
  themes for Twitter profile page,
    199–200
Chrome (Google), 22
Cohen, Marc (radio presenter), 8
Collier, Mack (blogger), 286
Collier, Marsha (author)
  contact information for, 8
  eBay For Dummies, 286
  eBay For Seniors For Dummies, 8
colourlovers (website), 199
comments
  on friend's status in Facebook, 134
  leaving on Flixster, 283–284
communicating, Twitter
  about, 203
  favorite tweets, 208–209
  guidelines for, 204–206
  retweeting (RT), 206–208
  topics for tweets, 209–214
communicating with Group
    members (Facebook), 167–170
composing Gmail messages, 59–61
Computer and Technology Show
    (radio show), 8

computers
  about, 11–12
  browsers, 12, 21–26
  hardware, 12–19
  shopping for, 19–21
  uploading photos from, 252–253
configuring wireless networks, 40–41
confirming Facebook account, 90
connections, Facebook
  about, 115
  chatting with friends, 130–132
  commenting on friend's status, 134
  connecting with Facebook networks, 125–127
  Facebook Search, 118–121
  finding friends in other friends' lists, 122–123
  Navigation bar, 116–118
  posting notes, 135–136
  posting updates on friend's walls, 132–133
  removing messages from wall, 136
  responding to friend requests, 123–125
  retrieving private messages, 129–130
  sending friend requests, 121–122
  sending private messages to friends, 127–129
connections, Internet
  about, 27
  broadband, 28–30, 32–34
  cable, 30
  dial-up, 28, 31–32
  Powerline network, 34–36
  wireless network (WiFi), 36–41

connections, Twitter, 230–232
contact information, on Facebook, 95
contacts, adding to Gmail, 57–59
Contour Mouse (Contour Design), 18–19
conventions, explained, 4–5
copying URLs of videos, 114
cost
  Flickr Pro member, 73
  Hotmail, 49
  monitors, 19
  Powerline network, 34
  Yahoo! Mail, 47
Costco.com (website), 19
Cover photo (Facebook), 105–107
CPU (central processing unit), 17
creating
  event invitations, 170–172
  photo albums on Facebook, 141–145
Creative Commons, 244–245
crediting websites and people, 242–245
crowd-sourcing
  about, 263–264
  Amazon, 265–267
  Angie's List, 264–265
  Flixster, 282–284
  review tips, 274–276
  TripAdvisor, 276–281
  Yelp, 267–273
custombackgroundsfortwitter (website), 199
#custserv hashtag, 227

• D •

D command, 202
data plans, 189
deleting
  photos in Facebook, 150
  posts in Facebook, 110–111
  status updates in Facebook,
    110–111
desktop computer, 12
dial-up connection, 28, 31–32
Digital Subscriber Line (DSL), 29
direct message (DM), 201, 202, 205
DJs, online, 254–258
DM (direct message), 201, 202, 205
#dogtalk chat, 228
domain address, 43
drive
  CD/DVD, 18
  flash, 17
  hard, 16–17
DSL (Digital Subscriber Line), 29

• E •

#earthquake hashtag, 227
eBay For Dummies (Collier), 286
eBay For Seniors For Dummies
  (Collier), 8
editing Facebook profiles, 96
802.11a, 38
802.11b, 38, 39
802.11g, 38, 39
802.11n, 38–39
e-mail
  about, 43–44
  adding contacts to Gmail, 57–59
  composing in Gmail, 59–61

Gmail account setup, 52–57
  options, 44–46
  passwords, 51–52
  phishing, 41
  photos, 253
  sending, 59–61
  web-based providers, 46–51
e-mail links, 41–42
encryption, 39, 80
Entertainment Weekly (magazine), 71
ergonomic mouse, 18
Ethernet bridge, 35
Ethernet network, 33
event administrator, 172
Events (Facebook)
  about, 153–154
  adding to Timeline, 112–113
  creating invitations, 170–172
  exporting to calendars, 173–174
  reviewing, 172–173
exporting Facebook events to
    calendars, 173–174
external hard drive, 17

• F •

Facebook. *See also specific topics*
  about, 64–66, 79–80
  account sign up, 80–82
  adding events to Timeline,
    112–113
  adding personal information,
    84–85
  adding photos to Timeline,
    111–112
  age, 81
  Application Directory, 176
  apps, 154, 174–179

@ sign used in, 133
browsing, 176–179
chats, 130–132
commenting on friend's status, 134
communicating with Group members, 167–170
confirming account, 90
connections. *See* connections, Facebook
contact information, 95
Cover photo, 105–107
creating photo albums, 141–145
editing profile, 96
Events. *See* Events (Facebook)
exporting events to calendars, 173–174
filling out profile information, 91–95
finding friends, 82–83, 118–121
finding pages, 154–159
Friend Requests icon, 116
Friends box, 107
games, 153–154, 174–179
Groups. *See* Groups (Facebook)
groups administrator, 167
Home page, 102–104
Likes box, 108
Map box, 107–108
Messages icon, 116
Notifications icon, 116
Pages, 154–159
Photos box, 107
Places, 157–158
posting videos to profile page, 260
privacy, 98–102, 135, 139
Search, 118–121

security controls, 42
Security settings, 98–102
sending video links as messages to friends, 260–261
sharing information. *See* sharing, Facebook
signing up for accounts, 80–82
tagging photos, 146–148
Timeline page, 104–108, 111–113
untagging photos, 149–150
uploading photos, 85–89, 137–141
uploading profile photos, 85–89
videos. *See* videos
Facebook blog (website), 98
factory-refurbished computer, 20
Farmville 2, 178
FAV command, 202
favorite tweets, 208–209
FF, 226–230
#FF hashtag, 227
filling out profile information in Facebook, 91–95
finding
  friends in other friends' lists, 122–123
  friends on Facebook, 82–83, 118–121
  friends with Facebook Search, 118–121
  hotel reviews on TripAdvisor, 276–278
  movies on Flixster, 282–283
  nightlife on Yelp, 268–270
  pages on Facebook, 154–159
  people to follow on Twitter, 188–193

finding *(continued)*
  restaurants on Yelp, 268–270
  shopping on Yelp, 268–270
  trends with Summize, 222–225
  videos on YouTube, 258–262
Firefox
  about, 21
  menus, 24
  shortcuts, 26
5GHz band, 38–39
flash drive, 17
Flash Player (Adobe), 140
Flickr, 73
Flixster
  finding movies on, 282–283
  leaving comments on, 283–284
FOLLOW command, 202
FollowFriday, 226–230
FollowFriday hashtag, 227
formats, wireless, 38–39
forward slash (/), 220
Friend Finder, 120–121
Friend Requests icon (Facebook),
  116
friends
  chatting with in Facebook,
    130–132
  commenting on status of on
    Facebook, 134
  finding in other friends' lists,
    122–123
  finding on Facebook, 82–83,
    118–121
  finding with Facebook Search,
    118–121
  ignoring friend requests, 125
  posting update on walls of,
    132–133

  responding to friend requests,
    123–125
  sending friend requests, 121–122
  sending private messages in
    Facebook, 127–129
  sending video links as messages
    to, 260–261
  viewing lists of, 235–238
Friends box (Facebook), 107

• *G* •

games (Facebook), 153–154,
  174–179
#gardenchat chat, 228
GB (gigabytes), 16–17
GET command, 202
gigabytes (GB), 16–17
Gmail
  about, 49–51, 289
  account sign up, 52–57
  adding contacts, 57–59
  composing messages, 59–61
Google Blogger, 289
Google Calendar, 50
Google Chat, 49
Google Chrome, 22
Google+ For Dummies (Stay), 291
Google Mail
  about, 49–51, 289
  account sign up, 52–57
  adding contacts, 57–59
  composing messages, 59–61
Google profile, 249
Gottlieb, Jessica (blogger), 287
Groups (Facebook)
  about, 153–154
  administrator, 167

communicating with members, 167–170

joining, 159–162

starting, 162–167

• *H* •

hard drive, 16–17

hardware

  options, 16–19

  selecting, 12–16

hashtags (#), 209, 226–230

highlighting text, 60–61

Home page (Facebook), 102–104

hotel reviews

  adding on TripAdvisor, 278–281

  finding on TripAdvisor, 276–278

Hotmail (Microsoft), 48–49

hotspots, 39

Hulu, 75–76

• *I* •

Iannolo, Jennifer (CEO), 230

icons

  Facebook, 116

  license, 244–245

ignoring friend requests, 125

images

  e-mailing, 253

  posting to blogs, 293–300

  profile, 85–89

  resizing on blogs, 298

  sharing on Flickr, 73

  sharing with Twitpic, 250–254

  uploading from computers, 252–253

  uploading to blogs from mobile phones, 296

images, Facebook

  about, 137

  adding to Timeline, 111–112

  creating albums, 141–145

  deleting, 150

  tagging, 146–148

  untagging yourself in, 149–150

  uploading for profile, 85–89

  uploading to accounts, 137–141

images, Twitter, 213–214

Instant Messenger service, for Hotmail accounts, 49

instant synchronizing feature, with Gmail, 50

Internet connections

  about, 27

  broadband, 28–30, 32–34

  cable, 30

  dial-up, 28, 31–32

  Powerline network, 34–36

  wireless network (WiFi), 36–41

Internet Explorer (Microsoft)

  about, 21

  menus, 24

  shortcuts, 25

Internet resources

  Amazon, 19, 266

  Angie's List, 264

  Application Directory (Facebook), 176

  author, 8

  BestBuy.com, 19

  Bing, 274

  bit.ly, 246

  blip.fm, 254

  broadband connections, 28

  Buy.com, 19

  colourlovers, 199

Internet resources *(continued)*
  Contour Design, 18
  Costco.com, 19
  crediting, 242–245
  custombackgroundsfortwitter, 199
  DSL, 29
  Facebook, 80
  Facebook blog, 98
  Firefox, 23
  Flixster, 282
  free WiFi, 31
  Friend Finder, 121
  Gmail, 52, 289
  Google Blogger, 289
  Google profile, 249
  Jessica Gottlieb's blog, 287
  Mack Collier's blog, 286
  Marsha Collier's blog, 287
  Microsoft Hotmail, 48
  Microsoft Internet Explorer, 23
  OAuth, 251
  outlet stores, 20
  Seesmic, 237
  Summize, 222
  tinyurl.com, 246
  TripAdvisor, 276
  TweetChat, 228
  TweetDeck, 237
  twitbacks, 199
  Twitpic, 250
  Twitter, 184
  twitterbackgrounds, 199
  Twubs, 228
  WeFollow, 216
  What the Hashtag?, 226, 228
  Yahoo! Mail, 47
  Yelp, 268
  YouTube, 258

invitations, events (Facebook),
    170–172
ISP (Internet Service Provider)
  about, 27
  e-mail addresses from, 44–45
  selecting, 28–31

• *J* •

#jobs chat, 229
joining Facebook Groups, 159–162
#journchat chat, 228

• *K* •

KB (kilobytes), 87
keyboards
  options, 18
  size, 13
kilobytes (KB), 87

• *L* •

laptops, 12–15
LCD (Liquid Crystal Display), 19
license icons (Creative Commons),
    244–245
Likes box (Facebook), 108
LinkedIn, 69–70
links
  e-mail, 41–42
  length of, 245–249
  video, 260–261
Liquid Crystal Display (LCD), 19
locating
  friends in other friends' lists,
    122–123
  friends on Facebook, 82–83,
    118–121

friends with Facebook Search, 118–121

hotel reviews on TripAdvisor, 276–278

movies on Flixster, 282–283

nightlife on Yelp, 268–270

pages on Facebook, 154–159

people to follow on Twitter, 188–193

restaurants on Yelp, 268–270

shopping on Yelp, 268–270

trends with Summize, 222–225

videos on YouTube, 258–262

• M •

Mafia Wars, 179

mail transfer agent (MTA), 44

Map box (Facebook), 107–108

media-card reader, 18

menus, 24

messages
  Facebook wall, 136
  text, 50, 66

messages, e-mail
  about, 43–44
  adding contacts to Gmail, 57–59
  composing in Gmail, 59–61
  Gmail account setup, 52–57
  options, 44–46
  passwords, 51–52
  phishing, 41
  photos, 253
  sending, 59–61
  web-based providers, 46–51

Messages icon (Facebook), 116

Microsoft Hotmail, 48–49

Microsoft Internet Explorer
  about, 21
  menus, 24
  shortcuts, 25

MIMO (multiple-input multiple-output) technology, 38

mobile phones, uploading photos to blogs from, 296

modem, 34

monitors
  options, 19
  size, 13

mouse, 18

mouse over, 107

movies
  finding on Flixster, 282–283
  watching on Hulu, 75–76

Mozilla Firefox
  about, 21
  menus, 24
  shortcuts, 26

MTA (mail transfer agent), 44

multiple media-card reader, 18

multiple-input multiple-output (MIMO) technology, 38

music
  sharing on Twitter, 212
  streaming on Pandora, 73–75

Music Genome Project, 73

#musicmonday hashtag, 226

MySpace, 68–69

• N •

naming blogs, 291–293

Navigation bar, 116–118

Netbooks, 14–15

networks
  about, 32
  Facebook, 125–127
  types, 32–33
nightlife, finding on Yelp, 268–270
notebooks, 12–14
notes, posting in Facebook,
    135–136
notices (Twitter), 200–201
Notifications icon (Facebook), 116

• O •

OAuth protocol, 251
online DJs, 254–258
online retailers, buying computers
    from, 19
online storage, Hotmail, 49
ON/OFF command, 202
opinions, giving or taking
  about, 263–264
  Amazon, 265–267
  Angie's List, 264–265
  Flixster, 282–284
  review tips, 274–276
  TripAdvisor, 276–281
  Yelp, 267–273
outlet stores, 20
Outlook/Outlook Express, 49
overheards, sharing on Twitter, 213

• P •

Pages (Facebook), 154–159
Pandora, 73–75
passwords
  e-mail, 51–52
  Twitter, 185, 195–196

people
  connecting with on Twitter,
    230–232
  crediting, 242–245
  finding to follow on Twitter,
    188–193
personal information, adding to
    Facebook, 84–85
phishing e-mails, 41
photos
  e-mailing, 253
  posting to blogs, 293–300
  profile, 85–89
  resizing on blogs, 298
  sharing on Flickr, 73
  sharing with Twitpic, 250–254
  uploading from computers,
    252–253
  uploading to blogs from mobile
    phones, 296
photos, Facebook
  about, 137
  adding to Timeline, 111–112
  creating albums, 141–145
  deleting, 150
  tagging, 146–148
  untagging yourself in, 149–150
  uploading for profile, 85–89
  uploading to accounts, 137–141
photos, Twitter, 213–214
Photos box (Facebook), 107
Picasa Web Albums, 295
Places (Facebook), 157–158
planning blogs, 286–288
pointing device, 18
ports, USB, 17

posting
  notes in Facebook, 135–136
  photos to blogs, 293–300
  stories to blogs, 293–300
  updates on friend's walls, 132–133
  videos to Facebook profile page, 260
posts, deleting in Facebook, 110–111
Powerline network
  about, 33
  connecting, 34–36
pre-shared key (PSK) mode, 39
privacy, Facebook
  about, 98
  notes, 135
  photos, 139
  settings, 98–102
private messages
  retrieving in Facebook, 129–130
  sending to friends in Facebook, 127–129
profiles
  blogging, setting up, 300–303
  uploading photos to Facebook, 85–89
protecting tweets, 194–195
PSK (pre-shared key) mode, 39
#p2 hashtag, 227
public WiFi, 30–31

• Q •

questions, asking on Twitter, 212
#quote chat, 229
quotes, sharing on Twitter, 211–212

• R •

registering
  blogs, 289–291
  with Twitter, 184–188
  on Yelp, 270–272
removing messages from wall in Facebook, 136
resizing photos on blogs, 298
responding to friend requests, 123–125
restaurants, finding on Yelp, 268–270
retailers (online), buying computers from, 19
retrieving private messages in Facebook, 129–130
retweeting (RT), 206–208
reviewing upcoming Facebook events, 172–173
reviews
  hotel, 276–281
  leaving on Yelp, 272–273
  tips for, 274–276
router, 33–34, 40
RT (retweeting), 206–208
RT command, 202

• S •

Safari, 22
screen shots, 4
searching
  for tweeps on WeFollow, 216–221
  for tweeted topics, 209
security
  tips, 41–42
  wireless networks, 39

Security settings (Facebook), 98–102

Seesmic, 235–238

selecting
  broadband connection, 32–34
  hardware, 12–16
  ISP (Internet Service Provider), 28–31
  themes for Twitter profile page, 199–200

sending
  friend requests, 121–122
  Gmail messages, 59–61
  private messages to friends in Facebook, 127–129
  video links as messages to Facebook friends, 260–261

settings
  Privacy, Facebook, 98–102
  Security, Facebook, 98–102
  Twitter, account adjusting, 194–197

setup
  blogging profiles, 300–303
  dial-up connections, 31–32
  Powerline network, 35
  Twitter notices, 200–201

#sexonaplate chat, 229

sharing
  photos on Flickr, 73
  photos with Twitpic, 250–254
  videos on YouTube, 258–262

sharing, Facebook
  about, 97–98, 241
  adding photos to Timeline, 111–112
  adding Timeline life events, 112–113

blip, 256–258
credits, 242–245
deleting status, 110–111
Home page, 102–104
links, 245–249
online DJ, 254–256
Privacy settings, 98–102
Security Settings, 98–102
Timeline page, 104–108
TwitPic, 250–254
updating posts, 110–111
updating status, 109–110
YouTube, 258–262
YouTube videos, 113–114

sharing, Twitter
  about, 241
  blip, 256–258
  credits, 242–245
  links, 245–249
  music, 212
  online DJ, 254–256
  overheards, 213
  photos, 213–214
  quotes, 211–212
  TwitPic, 250–254
  YouTube, 258–262

shipping costs, 21

shopping
  for computers, 19–21
  finding on Yelp, 268–270

Short Message Service (SMS), 50, 66

shortcuts
  Firefox, 26
  Internet Explorer, 25

sign up
  for blogs, 288–289
  Facebook, 80–82
  Gmail accounts, 52–57

size
  Facebook Cover photo, 106–107
  keyboards, 13
  monitors, 13
SkyDrive function, 49
smartphones, 15–16, 189
SMS (Short Message Service), 50, 66
social media, prevalence of, 2
social networks
  BlogSpot, 71–72
  Facebook. *See* Facebook
  Flickr, 73
  Hulu, 75–76
  LinkedIn, 69–70
  MySpace, 68–69
  Pandora, 73–75
  Twitter. *See* Twitter
  YouTube, 70–71, 113–114,
    258–262
Social Security Number, 42
spam filter, with Gmail, 50
speed, Powerline network, 34
starting Facebook Groups, 162–167
status (Facebook)
  commenting on for friends, 134
  deleting updates, 110–111
  updating, 109–110
Stay, Jesse (author)
  Google+ For Dummies, 291
storage space
  Gmail, 49
  Hotmail, 48
stories, posting to blogs, 293–300
streaming music on Pandora,
    73–75
Summize, 222–225
#sxsw hashtag, 226

• T •

tagging photos in Facebook,
    146–148
#tcot hashtag, 227
Texas HoldEm Poker, 178
text, highlighting, 60–61
text messages, 50, 66
themes, selecting for Twitter profile
    page, 199–200
Timeline page, Facebook
  about, 104–108
  adding events, 112–113
  adding photos, 111–112
tinyurl.com, 246
#tlot hashtag, 227
tools, Twitter
  about, 215
  connecting with people, 230–232
  FF, 226–230
  FollowFriday, 226–230
  hashtags, 226–230
  Seesmic, 235–238
  Summize, 222–225
  TweetDeck, 235–238
  Twitter Lists, 232–235
  WeFollow, 216–222
touchpads, 18
trackballs, 18
trends, finding with Summize,
    222–225
TripAdvisor
  adding hotel reviews, 278–281
  finding hotel reviews, 276–278
  tips, 274–276
Trojan, 42
TV, watching on Hulu, 75–76

tweeps, searching for on WeFollow, 216–221

TweetChat (website), 228

TweetDeck, 235–238

tweets
  favorite, 208–209
  protecting, 194–195
  searching for topics, 209
  topics for, 209–214

twitbacks (website), 199

Twitpic, sharing photos with, 250–254

Twitter. *See also specific topics*
  about, 66–67, 183–184
  adjusting account settings, 194–197
  asking questions, 212
  @ sign used in, 204–205
  case sensitivity in searches, 209
  chats, 228
  communicating on, 203–214
  connections, 230–232
  finding people to follow, 188–193
  friends on, 42
  notices, 200–201
  passwords, 185, 195–196
  registering with, 184–188
  selecting themes for profile page, 199–200
  setting up notices, 200–201
  sharing music, 212
  sharing overheards, 213
  sharing photos, 213–214
  sharing quotes, 211–212
  sharing video on, 262
  shorthand, 201–202
  tools. *See* tools, Twitter
  uploading avatars, 197–198
  username, 185

Twitter Lists, 232–235

twitterbackgrounds (website), 199

2.4GHz band, 37–39

Twubs (website), 228

• U •

UNFOLLOW command, 202

Uniform Resource Locator (URL)
  about, 4
  copying of videos, 114
  uploading photos to blogs from, 296

untagging photos, 149–150

updating
  posting on friend's walls, 132–133
  status in Facebook, 109–110

uploading
  avatars, 197–198
  photos from computers, 252–253
  photos to blogs from mobile phones, 296
  photos to Facebook, 137–141
  profile photos to Facebook, 85–89
  videos to Facebook, 114, 150–152

URL (Uniform Resource Locator)
  about, 4
  copying of videos, 114
  uploading photos to blogs from, 296

URL-shortening applications, 246

USB flash drive, 17

USB port, 17

username (Twitter), 185

• V •

videos
  copying URLs, 114
  finding on YouTube, 258–262
  posting to Facebook profile page,
    260
  sending links as messages to
    Facebook friends, 260–261
  sharing from YouTube on
    Facebook, 113–114
  sharing on YouTube, 258–262
  uploading to Facebook, 150–152
viewing friend's lists, 235–238

• W •

warranties, on factory-refurbished
    computers, 20
watching TV/movies on Hulu,
    75–76
Web-based e-mail services, 45–51
webcams, 140, 296
websites
  Amazon, 19, 266
  Angie's List, 264
  Application Directory (Facebook),
    176
  author, 8
  BestBuy.com, 19
  Bing, 274
  bit.ly, 246
  blip.fm, 254
  broadband connections, 28
  Buy.com, 19
  colourlovers, 199
  Contour Design, 18

  Costco.com, 19
  crediting, 242–245
  custombackgroundsfortwitter, 199
  DSL, 29
  Facebook, 80
  Facebook blog, 98
  Firefox, 23
  Flixster, 282
  free WiFi, 31
  Friend Finder, 121
  Gmail, 52, 289
  Google Blogger, 289
  Google profile, 249
  Jessica Gottlieb's blog, 287
  Mack Collier's blog, 286
  Marsha Collier's blog, 287
  Microsoft Hotmail, 48
  Microsoft Internet Explorer, 23
  OAuth, 251
  outlet stores, 20
  Seesmic, 237
  Summize, 222
  tinyurl.com, 246
  TripAdvisor, 276
  TweetChat, 228
  TweetDeck, 237
  twitbacks, 199
  Twitpic, 250
  Twitter, 184
  twitterbackgrounds, 199
  Twubs, 228
  WeFollow, 216
  What the Hashtag?, 226, 228
  Yahoo! Mail, 47
  Yelp, 268
  YouTube, 258

WeFollow
  adding yourself to, 221–222
  searching for tweeps on, 216–221
WEP (Wired Equivalent Privacy), 39
What the Hashtag? (website),
    226, 228
WiFi (Wireless Fidelity). *See*
    wireless networks (WiFi)
WiFi hotspots, 39
WiFi Protected Access (WPA), 39
Wired Equivalent Privacy (WEP), 39
Wireless Fidelity (WiFi), 30–31
wireless networks (WiFi)
  about, 33
  configuring, 40–41
  connecting, 36–41
  public, 30–31
  security, 39
wireless router, 40

Words with Friends, 179
WPA (WiFi Protected Access), 39

• Y •

Yahoo! Mail, 46–47
Yahoo! Messenger, 46
Yelp
  finding restaurants, shopping and
    nightlife, 268–270
  leaving reviews, 272–273
  registering to leave reviews,
    270–272
YouTube
  about, 70–71
  finding and sharing videos on,
    258–262
  sharing videos on Facebook,
    113–114

Notes

Notes